BLAST OFF!

**LOOK INSIDE
SPECTACULAR SPACECRAFT**

Written by
Ben Elcomb

Illustrated by
Rômolo D'Hipólito

BLAST OFF!

LOOK INSIDE SPECTACULAR SPACECRAFT

CONTENTS

06 INTRODUCTION
08 What is a spacecraft?
10 Timeline up to 1999
12 Timeline 2000–present
14 The anatomy of a spacecraft
16 How spacecraft get into space

18 SATELLITES
20 Parts of a satellite
22 How does a satellite orbit Earth?
24 Early satellites
26 Guided by Galileo
28 Watching the weather
30 Climate observation

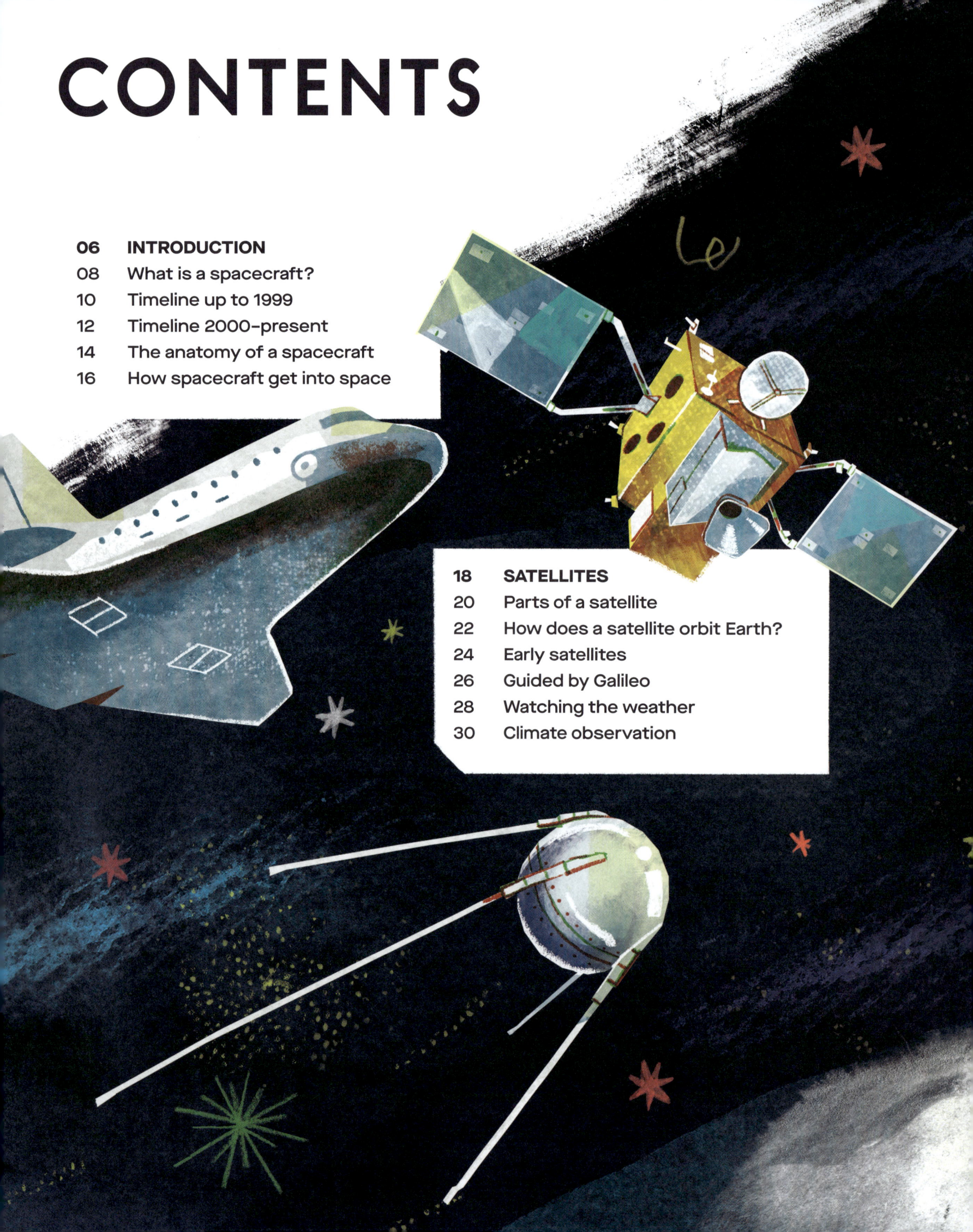

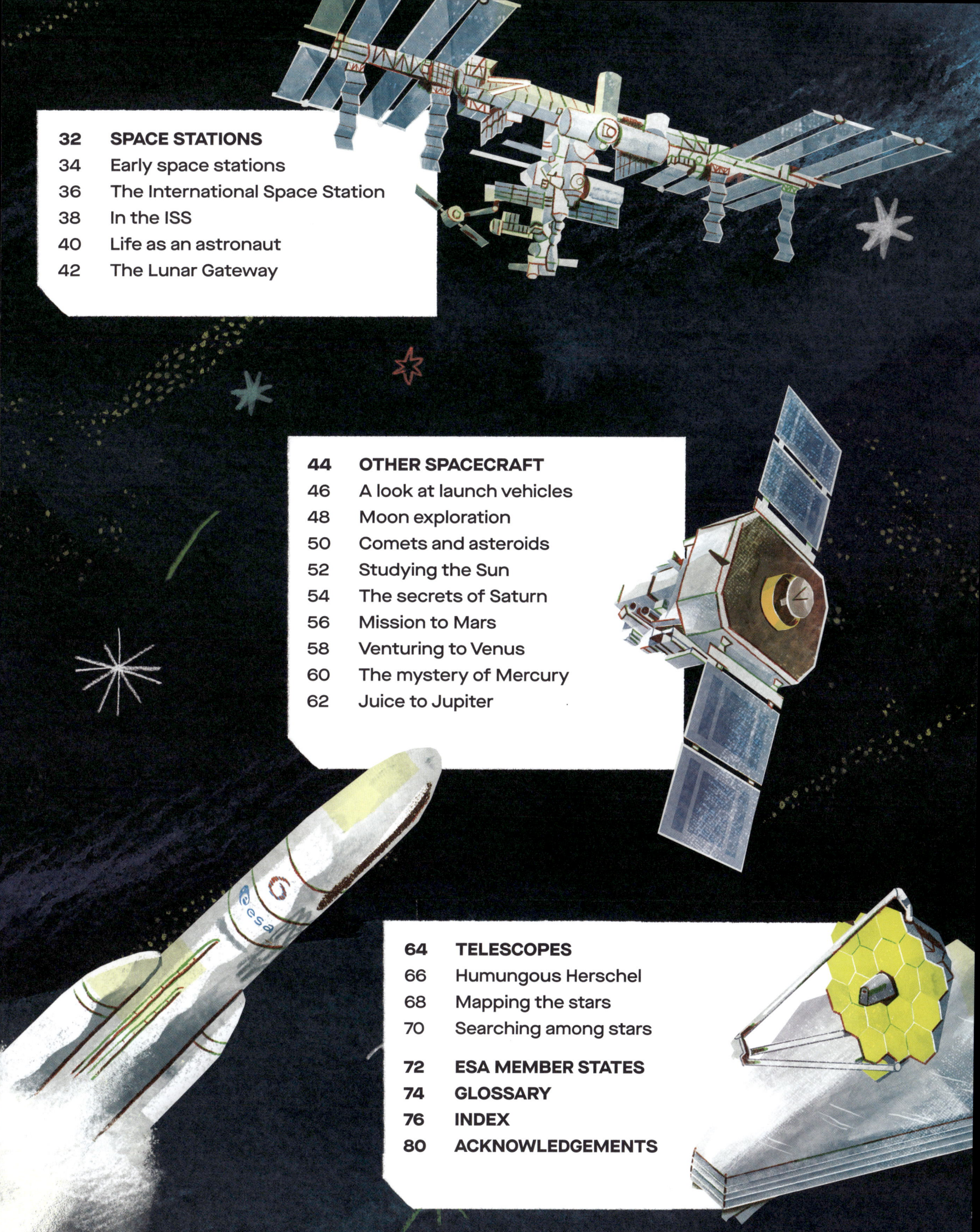

32 SPACE STATIONS
34 Early space stations
36 The International Space Station
38 In the ISS
40 Life as an astronaut
42 The Lunar Gateway

44 OTHER SPACECRAFT
46 A look at launch vehicles
48 Moon exploration
50 Comets and asteroids
52 Studying the Sun
54 The secrets of Saturn
56 Mission to Mars
58 Venturing to Venus
60 The mystery of Mercury
62 Juice to Jupiter

64 TELESCOPES
66 Humungous Herschel
68 Mapping the stars
70 Searching among stars

72 ESA MEMBER STATES
74 GLOSSARY
76 INDEX
80 ACKNOWLEDGEMENTS

INTRODUCTION

Space exploration has fascinated human beings for many years. To make this possible, various incredible vehicles, structures, and machines – with unique functions tailored to specific missions – have been designed.

WHAT IS A SPACECRAFT?

The term **spacecraft** refers to all types of vehicles and objects designed for space operations, with or without a human crew.

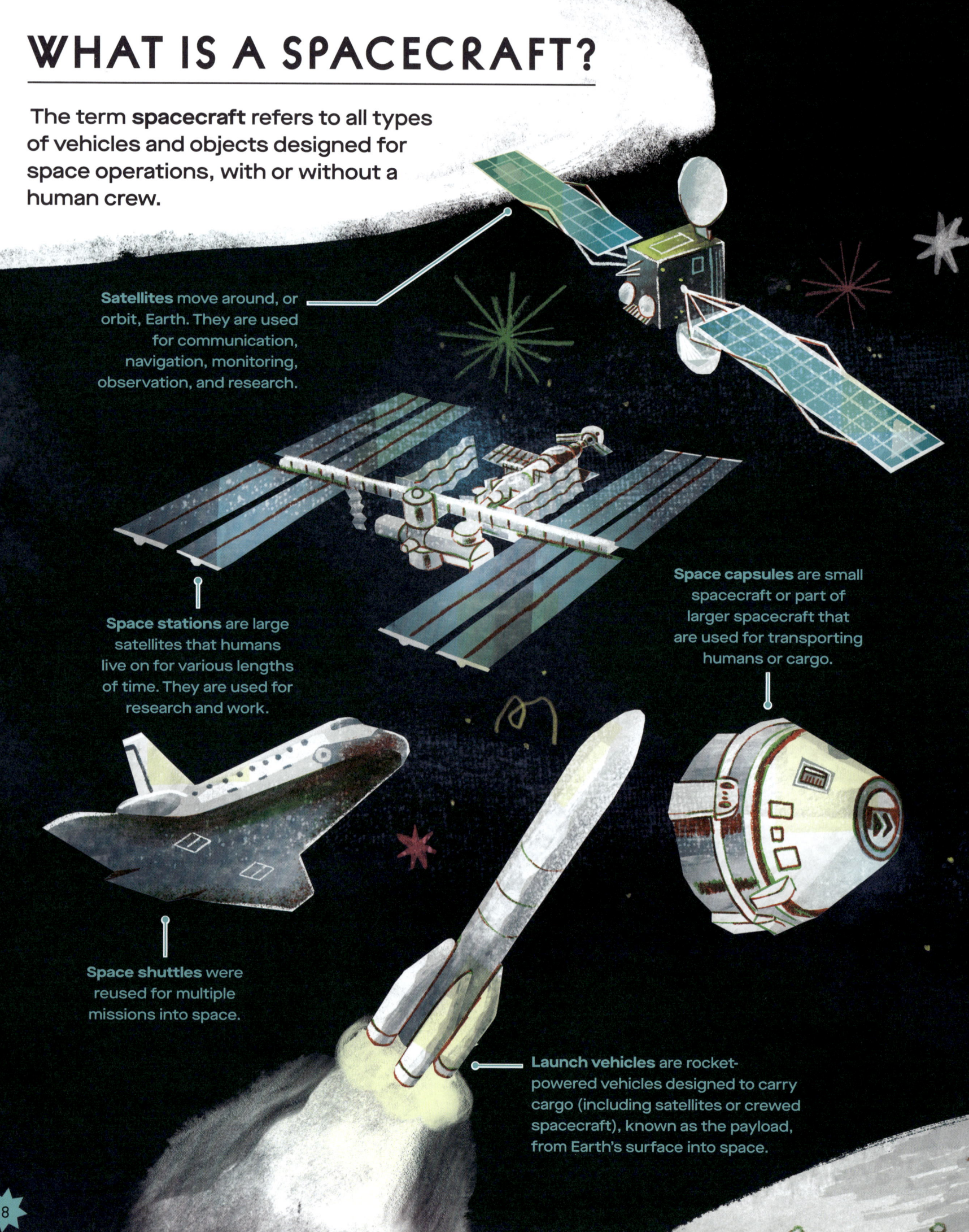

Satellites move around, or orbit, Earth. They are used for communication, navigation, monitoring, observation, and research.

Space stations are large satellites that humans live on for various lengths of time. They are used for research and work.

Space capsules are small spacecraft or part of larger spacecraft that are used for transporting humans or cargo.

Space shuttles were reused for multiple missions into space.

Launch vehicles are rocket-powered vehicles designed to carry cargo (including satellites or crewed spacecraft), known as the payload, from Earth's surface into space.

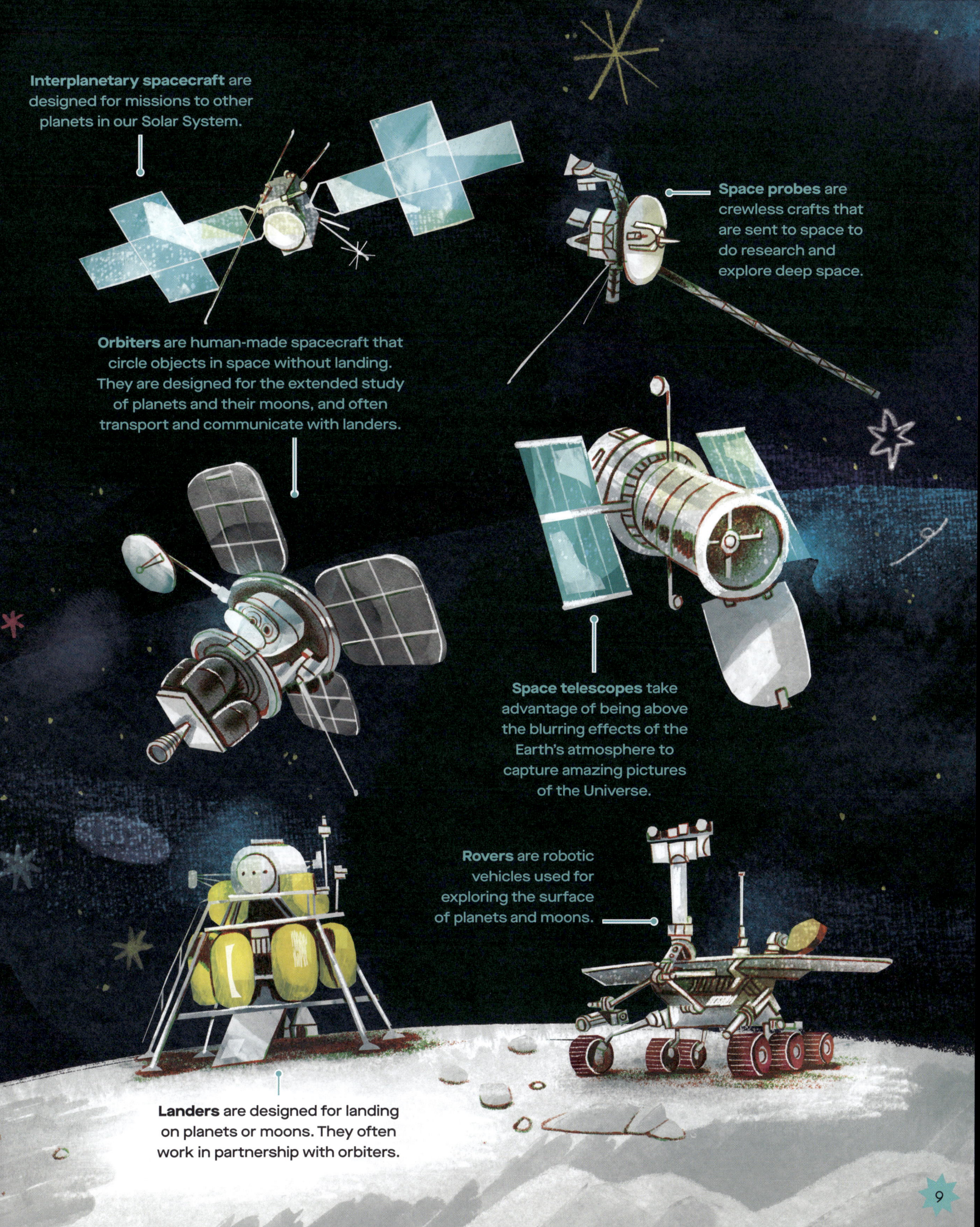

TIMELINE UP TO 1999

Records show that **astronomy** was one of the first-studied natural sciences, developed by early civilizations all over the globe.

Ancient astronomers could perform only limited investigations of the sky, using simple aids to the human eye. Space exploration took one giant leap with the invention of the telescope, then another in the twentieth century, as the first spacecraft were launched out of Earth's atmosphere.

Soviet spacecraft Luna 2 became the first spacecraft to reach the surface of the Moon.

Explorer 1 became the first US satellite, and the first satellite to carry science equipment.

Germany made the first spaceflight in history with the V-2 rocket.

1610 — 1903 — 1944 — 1949 — 1957 — 1958 — 1959

Italian astronomer and physicist Galileo Galilei discovered the moons of Jupiter using a homemade telescope.

Russian schoolteacher Konstantin Tsiolkovsky published a report entitled *Exploration of the Universe with Rocket Propelled Vehicles*. This report suggested that space exploration was possible using liquid fuel for rockets.

The Soviet Union launched Sputnik 1 – the first artificial satellite in space, and the first to send human-made signals back to Earth from space.

The USA sent a monkey called Albert II to space.

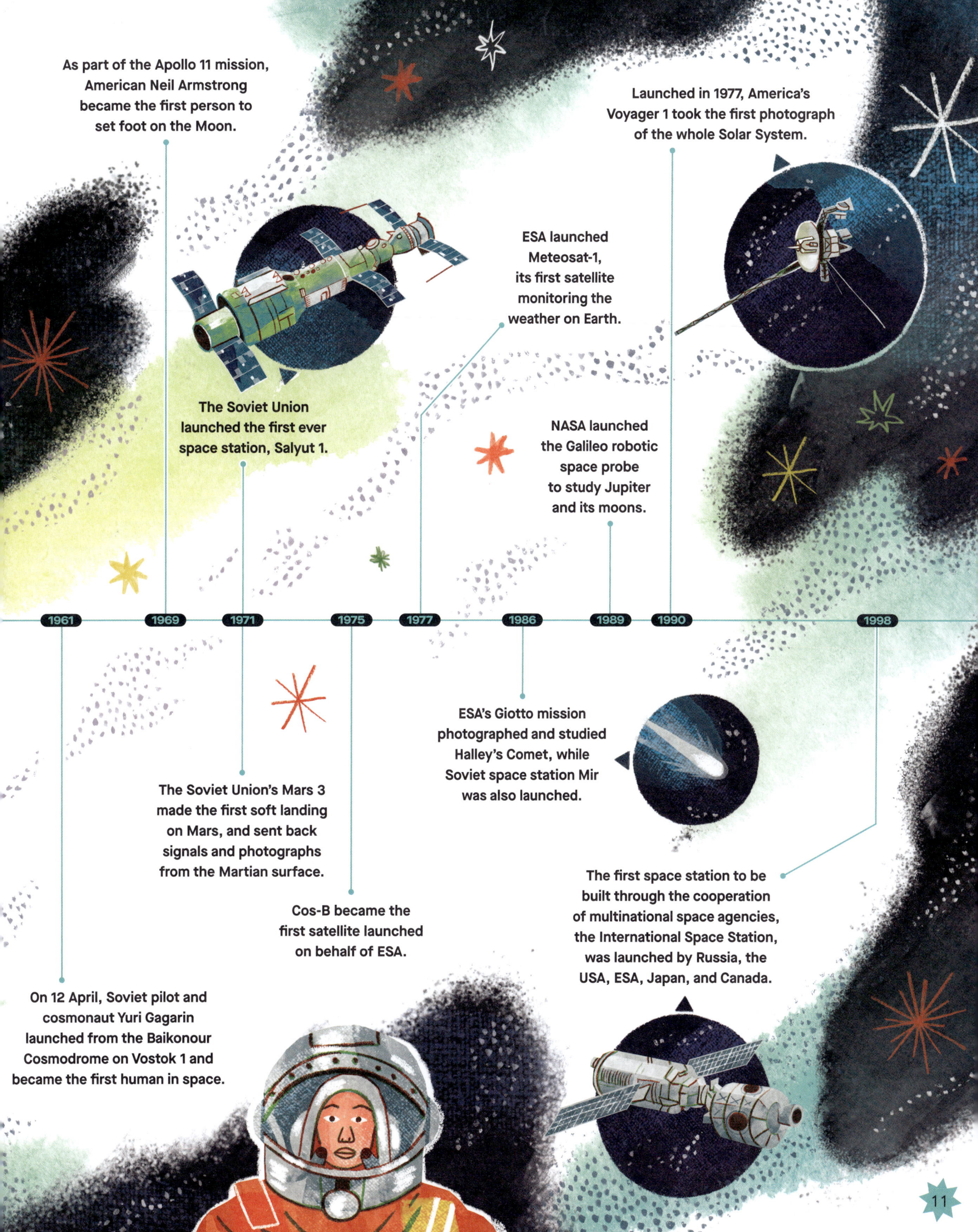

TIMELINE 2000–PRESENT

Spacecraft have developed even further this century, exploring remote places in our Solar System and beyond.

2001 — The NEAR Shoemaker mission became the first to land on an asteroid.

2004 — The first amateur rocket flight to reach space was made by CSXT GoFast.

2005 — Venus Express launched, becoming ESA's first Venus exploration mission.

2005 — The Cassini–Huygens mission made the first orbit of Saturn – a collaboration between NASA, ESA, and ASI.

2005 — ESA's Huygens landed on Titan, making it the first spacecraft to land on a moon other than Earth's.

2012 — NASA's Mars Science Laboratory became the first to use a sky crane to land on another planet. It used a platform with eight engines and three nylon tethers to softly deliver rovers to Mars.

2013 — Gaia – ESA's space observatory – launched, with the mission to map a billion local stars in 3D.

A joint project between the USA and Japan on the International Space Station saw the first food grown and eaten in space.

The James Webb Space Telescope, a joint project between NASA, ESA, and CSA, became the largest-ever space telescope.

NASA is currently working with ESA, CSA, and JAXA as partners on the Artemis programme, which will hopefully see the first crewed lunar landing since 1972 and establish a permanent base on the Moon, to facilitate future human missions to Mars.

BepiColombo was launched by ESA and JAXA to investigate Mercury, the innermost and least explored planet in the Solar System.

India's Chandrayaan-3 landed on our Moon's south polar region to study lunar water.

2015 — 2018 — 2020 — 2021 — 2023 — 2024 — PRESENT

The ESA Hera mission launched to visit the asteroid Didymos and its moon Dimorphos, as part of the NASA/ESA Asteroid Impact and Deflection Assessment (AIDA) collaboration.

Copernicus Sentinel-2A launched – a joint Earth observation mission between ESA and the European Commission that provides detailed coverage of land and coastal areas.

ESA's Solar Orbiter probe launched to observe the Sun.

THE ANATOMY OF A SPACECRAFT

While there are many types of spacecraft, most share some essential parts. These parts are divided into two sections of the spacecraft: **the service module,** which includes the engine, solar panels, navigation system, and communication system, and **the payload module,** which holds scientific instruments.

This is a pulled-apart view of BepiColombo (see pages 60–61).

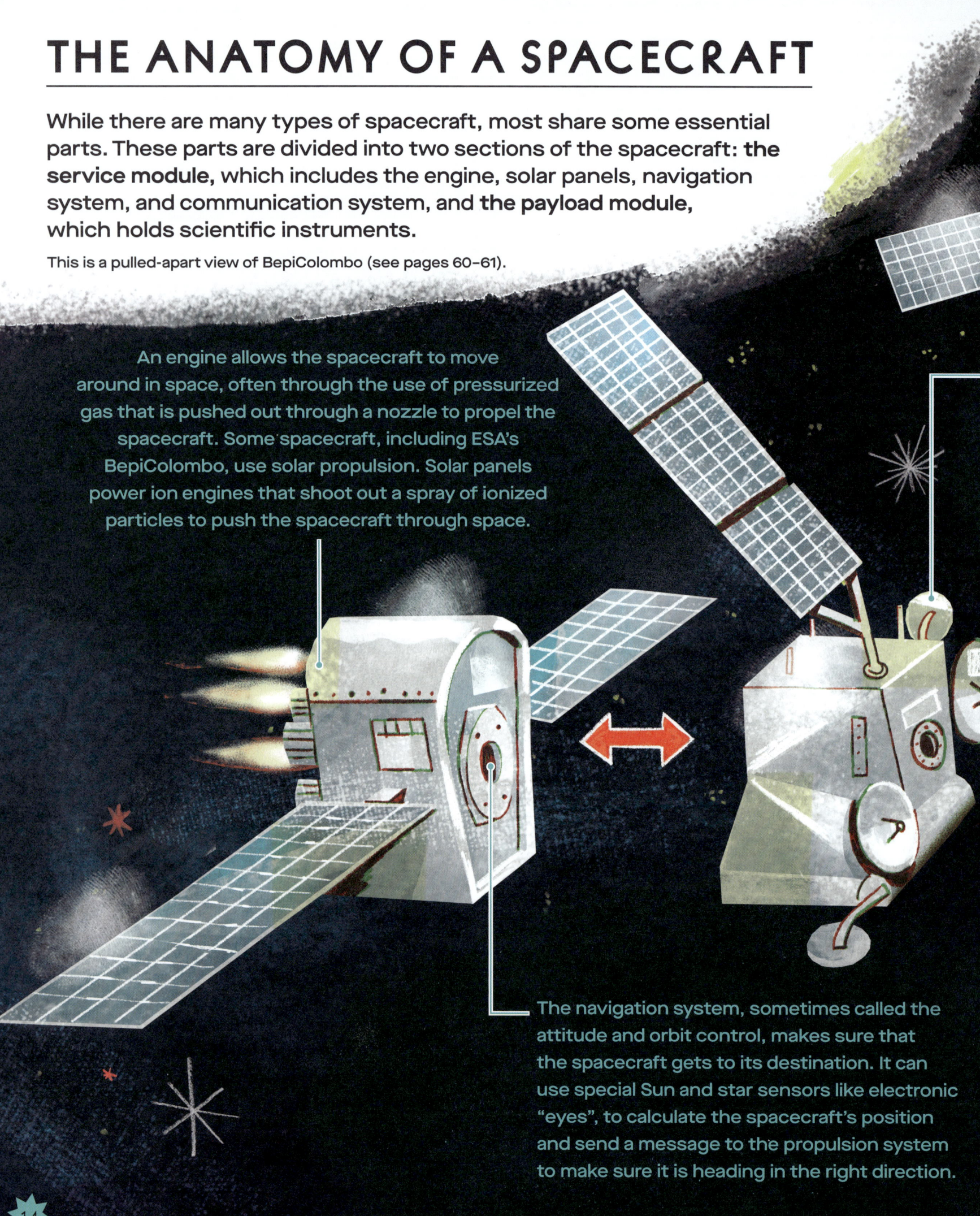

An engine allows the spacecraft to move around in space, often through the use of pressurized gas that is pushed out through a nozzle to propel the spacecraft. Some spacecraft, including ESA's BepiColombo, use solar propulsion. Solar panels power ion engines that shoot out a spray of ionized particles to push the spacecraft through space.

The navigation system, sometimes called the attitude and orbit control, makes sure that the spacecraft gets to its destination. It can use special Sun and star sensors like electronic "eyes", to calculate the spacecraft's position and send a message to the propulsion system to make sure it is heading in the right direction.

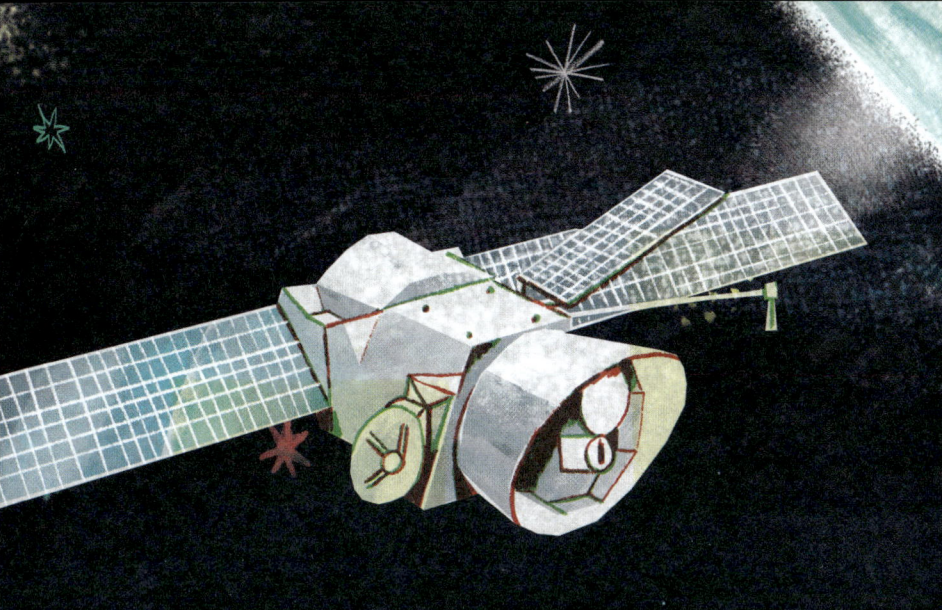

Payload modules contain scientific instruments – these vary depending on the mission, but can include equipment such as telescopes, cameras, and detectors. It can also contain crewed and autonomous landers that touch down on planets and moons. BepiColombo, a joint mission of ESA and JAXA, includes two payload modules.

Spacecraft often get their power from a collection of solar panels known as arrays. When the spacecraft is in eclipse or turned away from the Sun, batteries kick in to provide an alternative power source. This is known as the power subsystem.

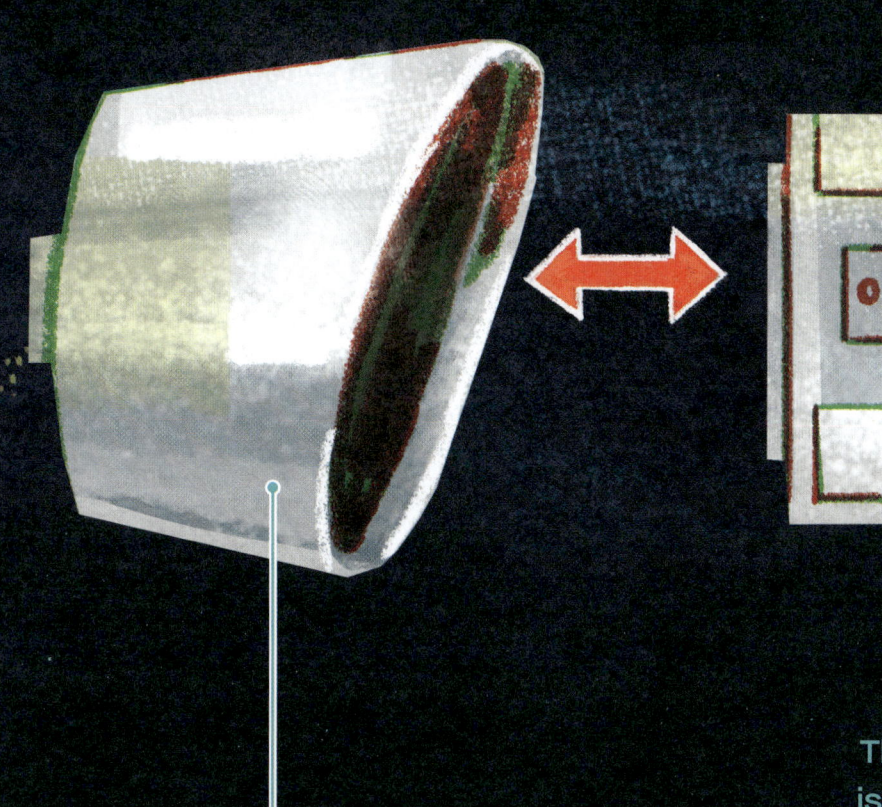

The sunshield is used to protect the spacecraft from the Sun's heat.

The communication system is made up of a combination of dishes and antennas that can receive instructions from Earth, and in return send scientific data to Earth.

HOW SPACECRAFT GET INTO SPACE

To get into space, we need to leave Earth. This might sound simple, but we can't just jump up and float into space because of something called gravity.

Ariane 6 lift off

Fighting gravity

Gravity is an invisible force that pulls everything towards Earth. Whenever you jump up, you are immediately pulled back down – this is gravity at work. To get into space, we need to fight against gravity. And to do this we need a vehicle with lots and lots of energy. This special vehicle is called a **rocket**.

Mighty force

A rocket engine burns a huge amount of fuel that is turned into hot gas. This gas is pushed out of the nozzle at high velocity. It pushes against Earth's gravity with such force that it propels the rocket upwards towards space. This force is called thrust.

To reach low Earth orbit, a rocket needs to produce enough thrust to make it travel at speeds of 29,000 km/h (18,000 mph). Most of a rocket's fuel is burned in the first few minutes!

Recreating rocket power

A similar effect can be achieved when you fill a balloon with air, but rather than tying it up you let it go. The air rushing out of the balloon makes it shoot off, just like a rocket blasting off.

SATELLITES

A satellite is an object that orbits something else. Moons, including our own, are satellites because they travel around planets. And Earth, and all the other planets in our Solar System, are satellites that travel around the Sun.

Artificial satellites are made by humans. They have various uses, including taking pictures of Earth, the Sun, and other planets, as well as providing communication and weather forecasting.

Even structures like the International Space Station can be described as a satellite.

PARTS OF A SATELLITE

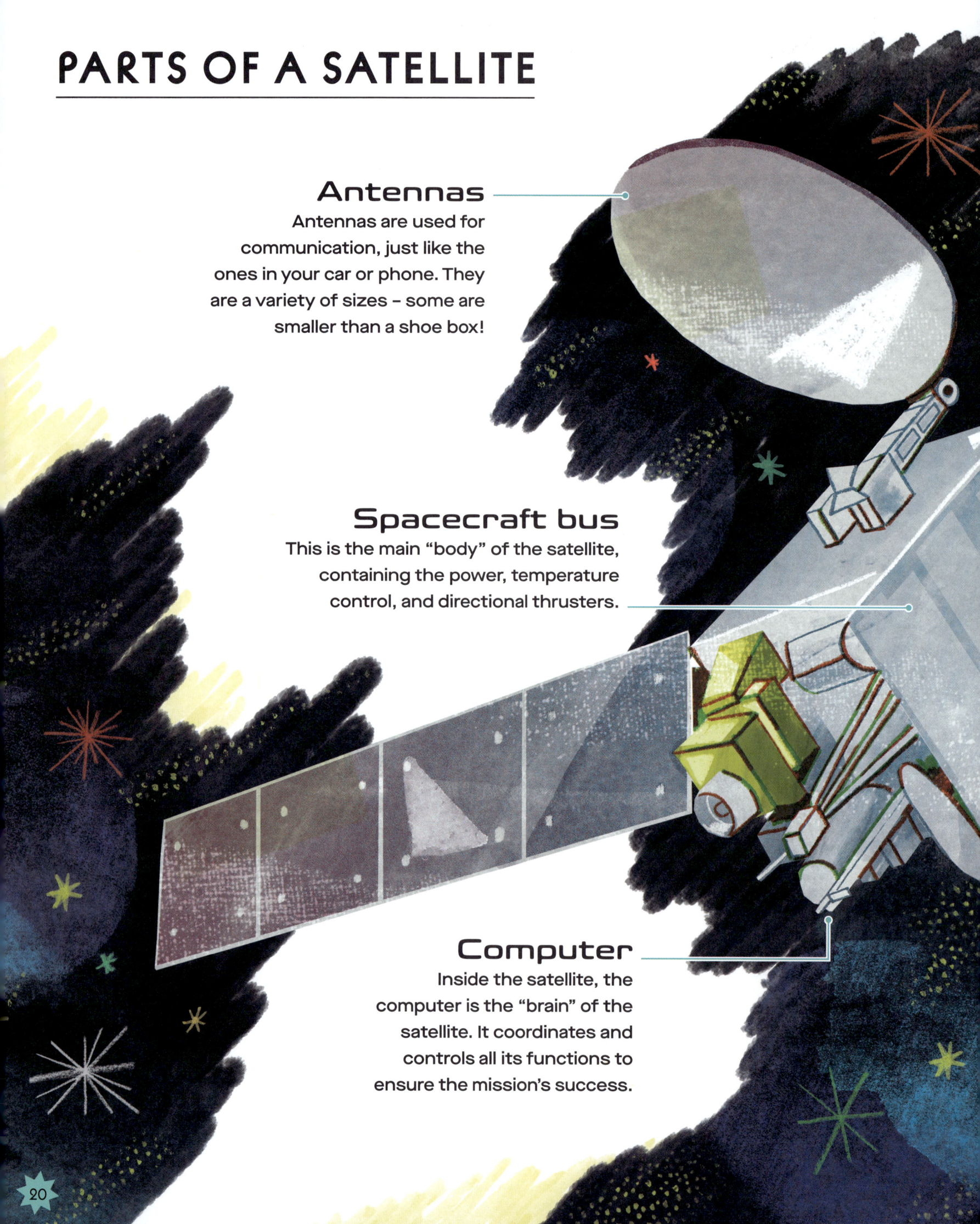

Antennas
Antennas are used for communication, just like the ones in your car or phone. They are a variety of sizes – some are smaller than a shoe box!

Spacecraft bus
This is the main "body" of the satellite, containing the power, temperature control, and directional thrusters.

Computer
Inside the satellite, the computer is the "brain" of the satellite. It coordinates and controls all its functions to ensure the mission's success.

Attitude and orbit control system

This controls the physical orientation of the satellite, in other words, which way it is pointing. Sensors, gyroscopes, and other components, which are inside the satellite, make sure it is always facing the right way, so that it can remain in communication with Earth and perform its mission.

Communication payload

This is the part of the satellite responsible for receiving, processing, and transmitting communication signals. Satellites contain multiple "channels", called transponders, which dictate how much information can be transmitted and how big the ground equipment must be to receive the signal.

Solar panels

These look like large "wings" on either side of the satellite. They convert solar energy from the Sun into electricity needed to power the satellite. Satellites also store power in rechargeable batteries, allowing them to work for years or even decades.

21

HOW DOES A SATELLITE ORBIT EARTH?

An orbit is a regular, repeating path that one object in space takes around another one. Different satellites orbit at different heights, or altitudes, above Earth's surface. These can be broken down into **three main types of orbit**.

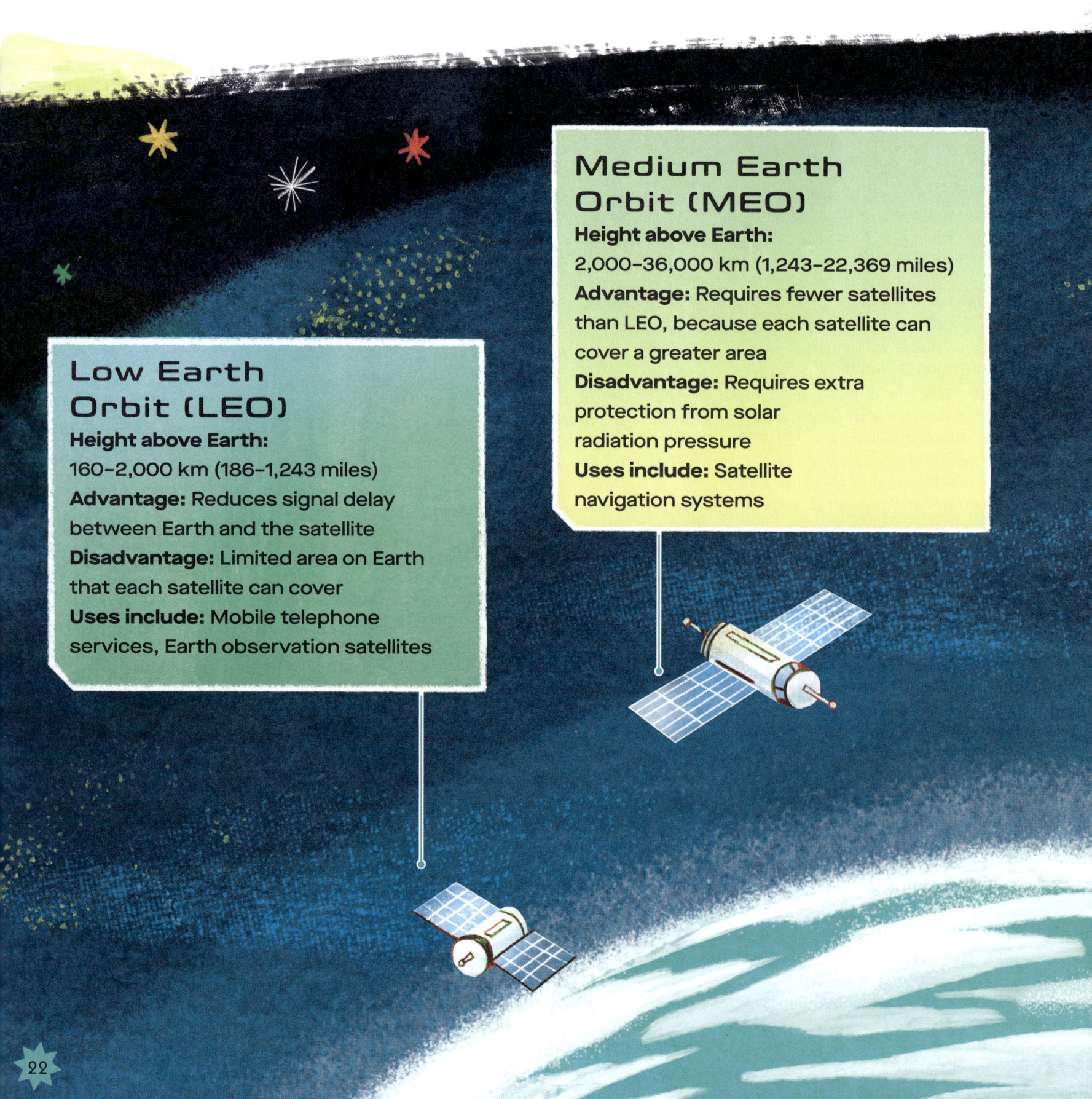

Low Earth Orbit (LEO)
Height above Earth: 160–2,000 km (186–1,243 miles)
Advantage: Reduces signal delay between Earth and the satellite
Disadvantage: Limited area on Earth that each satellite can cover
Uses include: Mobile telephone services, Earth observation satellites

Medium Earth Orbit (MEO)
Height above Earth: 2,000–36,000 km (1,243–22,369 miles)
Advantage: Requires fewer satellites than LEO, because each satellite can cover a greater area
Disadvantage: Requires extra protection from solar radiation pressure
Uses include: Satellite navigation systems

Geostationary Orbit (GEO)

Height above Earth: 36,000 km (22,369 miles)

Advantage: Only one GEO satellite is needed to provide connection to a fixed spot on Earth, and only three are needed at equal distances to provide coverage to the whole planet.

Disadvantage: Delay in signals due to large distance between Earth and satellite

Uses include: Television broadcasts, weather satellites

EARLY SATELLITES

Sputnik 1

The first artificial satellite was called Sputnik 1, and was launched by the Soviet Union in 1957. It consisted of a small aluminium ball – about the size of a beach ball – with four long antennas, and was battery-powered.

Sputnik contained radio transmitters that sent out a "beep, beep" sound, which was heard all over the world.

This small, but at the time impressive, satellite marked the beginning of a new exciting stage of the space age.

LOOK INSIDE

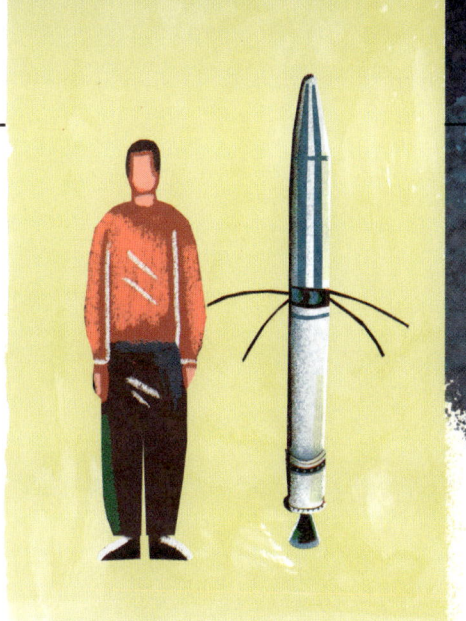

Explorer 1

NASA's first satellite, Explorer 1, launched in 1958.

Weighing just under 14 kg (31 lb), it was much lighter than Sputnik 1. It featured two antennas that transmitted scientific data to Earth.

Just like Sputnik 1, Explorer 1 was powered by batteries that made up around 40 per cent of the payload weight.

Cos-B

Launched on 9 August 1975 by ESA, Cos-B's primary objective was to study sources of gamma rays in the Universe.

Gamma rays are high energy waves of light and energy that speed through the Universe.

Cos-B is still regarded as one of the most successful space missions ever, and it helped to create an important map of the Milky Way called the 2CG catalogue.

GUIDED BY GALILEO

Galileo Galilei (1564–1642) was an Italian scientist who studied astronomy and navigation. This gives a clue as to what ESA's Galileo does – it is Europe's Global Navigation Satellite System (GNSS).

Galileo, like the US's GPS system, Russia's GLONASS system, and China's BeiDou (BDS), provides global positioning information.

Global navigation satellite systems have many uses on Earth. They can:

- Improve traffic flow
- Provide information for the exact position of any car, lorry, ship, or aircraft
- Help navigate remote places
- Make aircraft landings safer
- Guide people, including blind or partially sighted people
- Help search and rescue teams

The Galileo programme

Launched in 2011, Galileo first became operational in 2016. A joint initiative between the European Commisison and ESA, it now provides real-time positioning accurate to one metre without delay.

There are currently more than 30 satellites that make up the Galileo programme. They orbit at 23,222 km (14,429 miles) above Earth, and each weighs 675 kg (1,488 lb) – about the same as a cow. Each Galileo satellite is similar in size to a UK phone box.

It is estimated that Galileo has 3.5 billion users, including search and rescue teams who use it to save the lives of around 2,000 people each year.

Out of this world prize

Each satellite is named after a child who won a drawing competition set by the European Commission. One winner was chosen from each member state of the European Union, including Thijs from Belgium, Oriana from France, and Antonianna from Italy.

WATCHING THE WEATHER

Weather satellites help us forecast the weather on Earth. They study cloud, land, ocean, snow, and ice during the day and night. They can also help with climate studies, as well as recognize and predict dangerous weather, including dense fog, thunderstorms, gale-force winds, and intense rain.

Meteosat
The first Meteosat weather satellite was launched by the ESA in November 1977, 36,000 km (22,369 miles) above the Gulf of Guinea. A total of 12 Meteosats have been launched since then. Meteosat Second Generation (MSG) launched in 2002.

The third generation
Launched in 2022, the Meteosat Third Generation–Imager 1 (MTG-I) carries the Flexible Combined Imager and the Lightning Imager.

The **Flexible Combined Imager** helps to show what the weather is doing now and in the very near future (up to six hours). It is useful for looking at the impact of weather such as thunderstorms and fog. It can also monitor air quality and even improve fire detection.

The **Lightning Imager** continuously looks at lightning activity and can report on severe storms, and warn when and where lightning will strike. This can be especially useful for air navigation services close to airports.

Future Meteosat satellites

The MTG-S Sounding satellites will carry the latest high-tech equipment.

The Infrared Sounder will examine temperature and humidity in Earth's atmosphere, and provide data that helps to report on current and short-range weather forecasts.

As well as providing early warnings for thunderstorms, the new Sounder will also provide information on ozone, carbon monoxide, and volcanic ash composition in the atmosphere.

CLIMATE OBSERVATION

Satellites also play an important role in **environmental protection**, and are key tools for scientists when it comes to monitoring the climate.

Clever Copernicus

Copernicus is the Earth observation component of the European Union's Space programme. It provides valuable data that influences decisions in various industries, such as agriculture and forestry. It also plays a crucial role in addressing climate change and pollution, including monitoring marine litter. Additionally, Copernicus supports disaster relief efforts following natural events such as floods, volcanic eruptions, and wildfires.

Sentinel-2

The Copernicus programme includes the Sentinel-2 satellites, which provide scientists on Earth with amazing views from above. The mission consists of two identical satellites in the same orbit, 180 degrees apart from each other. Together they provide images of all Earth's land surface, large islands, inland waters, and coastal waters every five days.

Each satellite weighs 1.2 tonnes (1.3 tons) – that's about the same as a black rhino.

EarthCARE

The Earth Cloud Aerosol and Radiation Explorer (EarthCARE) is designed to help scientists understand more about how clouds and tiny particles in the air act as a barrier – regulating Earth's climate by reflecting the Sun's solar radiation back into space, as well as trapping infrared radiation emitted from Earth's surface. This information is crucial to helping scientists understand climate change.

Arctic Weather Satellite

The Arctic Weather Satellite (AWS) was launched to demonstrate how polar-orbiting satellites could help forecast weather in the Arctic and around the world. Carrying a single instrument, a microwave radiometer, the AWS measures temperature and humidity in the atmosphere – all from a height of 600 km (373 miles) above Earth.

SPACE STATIONS

A space station is a spacecraft that travels in a repeating loop, called a fixed orbit. Space stations provide somewhere for astronauts to live, sleep, and work for days or months at a time. Astronauts will often conduct experiments or collect scientific data while on board a space station.

EARLY SPACE STATIONS

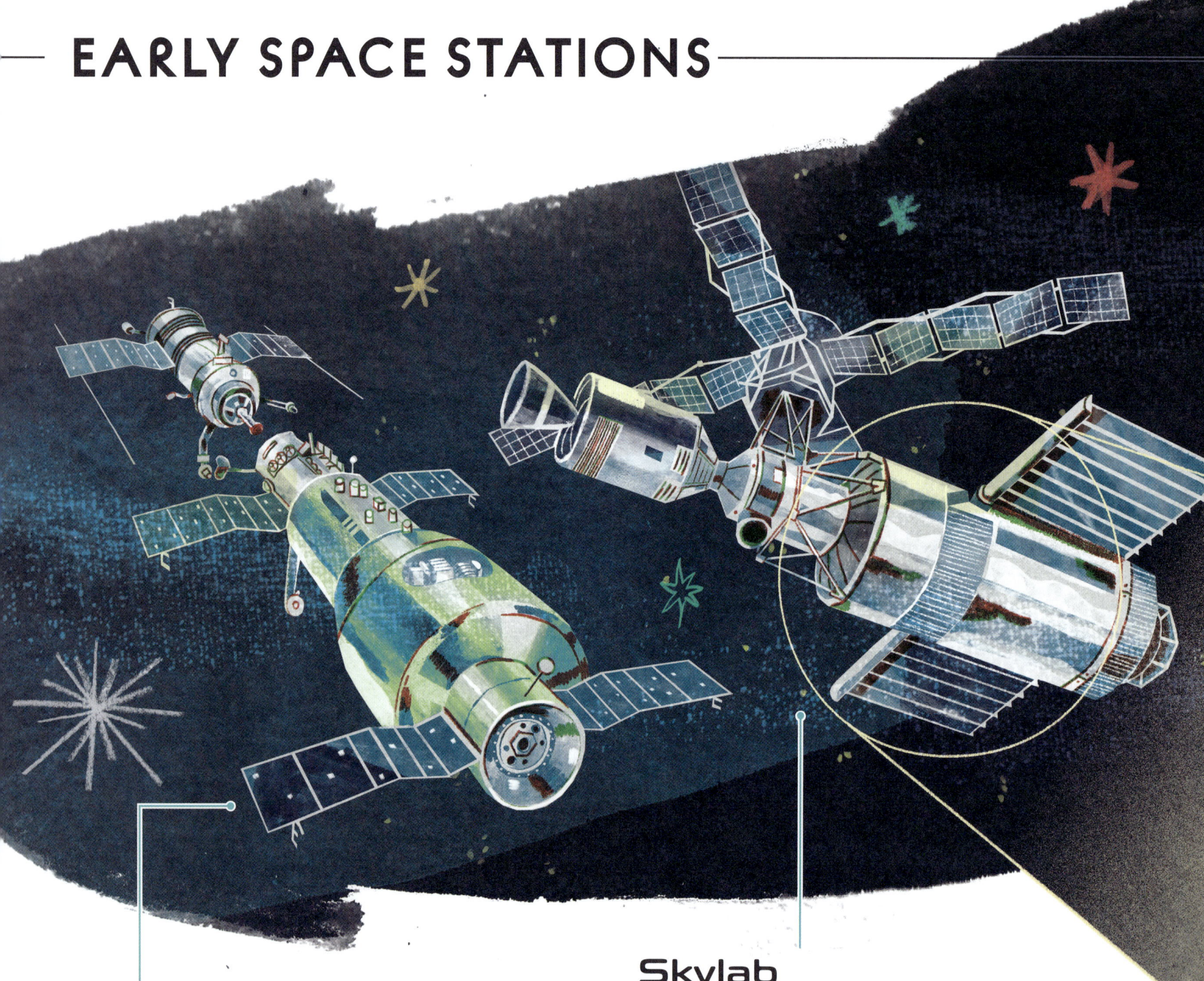

Salyut 1

The first space station was called Salyut 1, launched by the Soviet Union in April 1971.

Salyut 1 was intended to stay in orbit for an extended period, but after six months it faced several challenges including an electrical fire, which led to its premature re-entry into Earth's atmosphere.

Six more Salyut space stations were launched by the Soviety Union. The final one, Salyut 7, was in operation from 1982 until 1986.

Skylab

The first US space station was Skylab, launched in May 1973. It circled Earth once every 93 minutes at an altitude of 435 km (270 miles) above Earth.

Between 1973 and 1974, three crews, each made up of three people, spent over 171 days on Skylab. They took part in experiments involving Earth observation, engineering, and other scientific areas.

In July 1979, with the astronauts safely back on Earth, Skylab re-entered Earth's atmosphere and broke apart, with pieces landing in the Indian Ocean and in Southwest Australia.

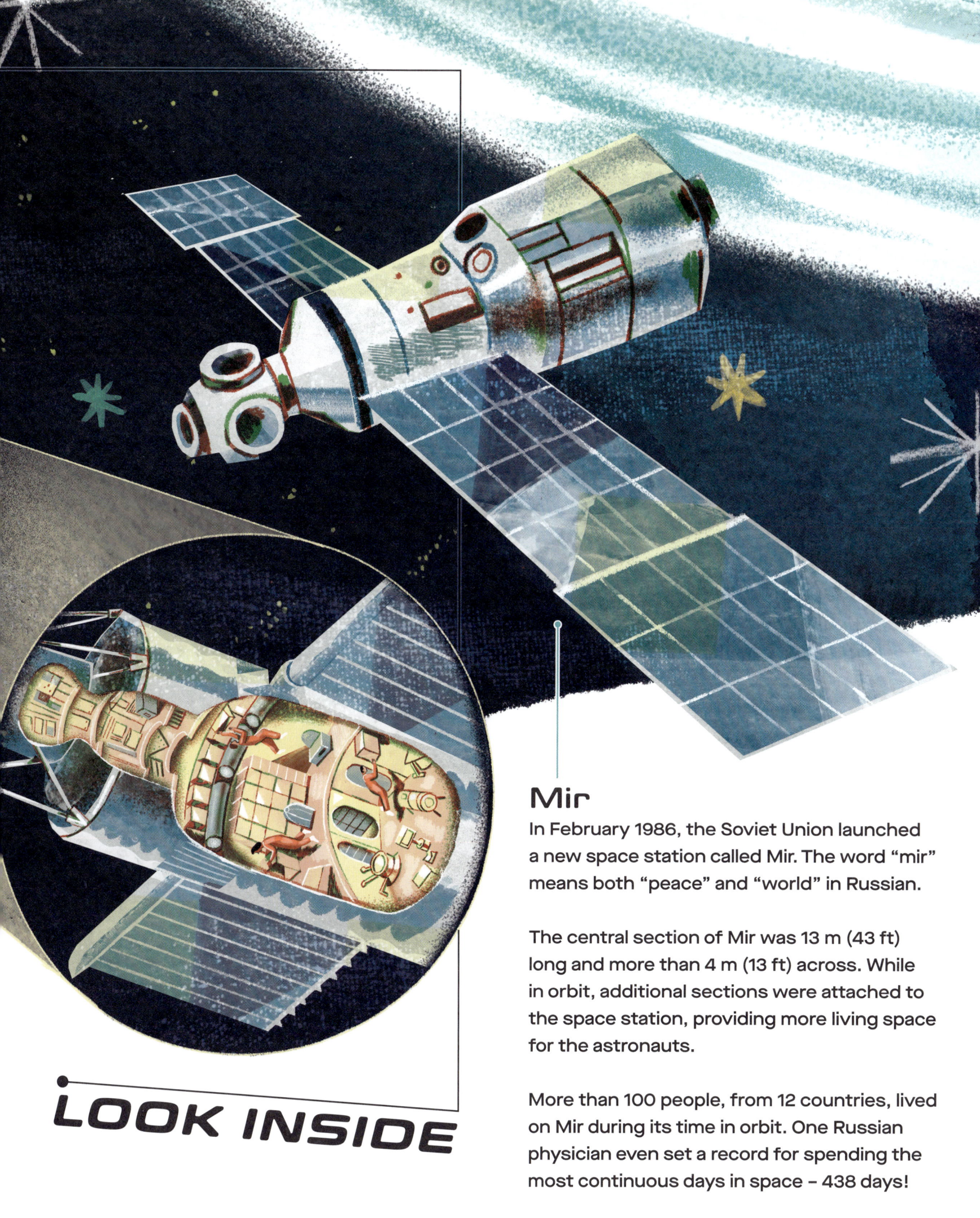

LOOK INSIDE

Mir

In February 1986, the Soviet Union launched a new space station called Mir. The word "mir" means both "peace" and "world" in Russian.

The central section of Mir was 13 m (43 ft) long and more than 4 m (13 ft) across. While in orbit, additional sections were attached to the space station, providing more living space for the astronauts.

More than 100 people, from 12 countries, lived on Mir during its time in orbit. One Russian physician even set a record for spending the most continuous days in space – 438 days!

THE INTERNATIONAL SPACE STATION

The International Space Station (ISS) is the biggest structure ever flown in space. Together, 27 countries worked to build it, including the USA, Russia, Canada, Japan, and 23 ESA member states.

The ISS can house a crew of six people, plus visitors, who live, work, eat, exercise, and sleep in space. It travels at an average speed of 27,000 km/h (16,777 mph) and orbits the Earth 16 times per day. At an altitude of about 400 km (250 miles), the ISS can be seen from Earth at night and looks like a shooting star.

Visiting spacecraft carrying crews and supplies connect to the ISS through docking ports.

Zveda is a Russian module with space for two astronauts to sleep, as well as some exercise equipment, a fridge and freezer, and a toilet.

The **Integrated Truss Structure** acts as a backbone for the ISS, to which a number of modules are attached where astronauts live and work.

1983	1984	1988	1993	1998
The USA and its partners in Europe, Japan, and Canada discussed a joint space station.	President Reagan tasked NASA with developing a permanently crewed space station.	NASA and ESA agreed on cooperation in the design and development of the space station.	The USA and Russia agreed to work together on human spaceflight activities.	The first piece of the ISS was launched. It was called Zarya, which means "sunrise" in Russian.

2020	2011	2009	2008	2001	2000
SpaceX Dragon 2 was the first private spacecraft to take people to the ISS.	Construction of the ISS was completed.	The ISS became fully operational.	ESA's Columbus laboratory became part of the ISS.	The first European astronaut arrived.	The first crew arrived.

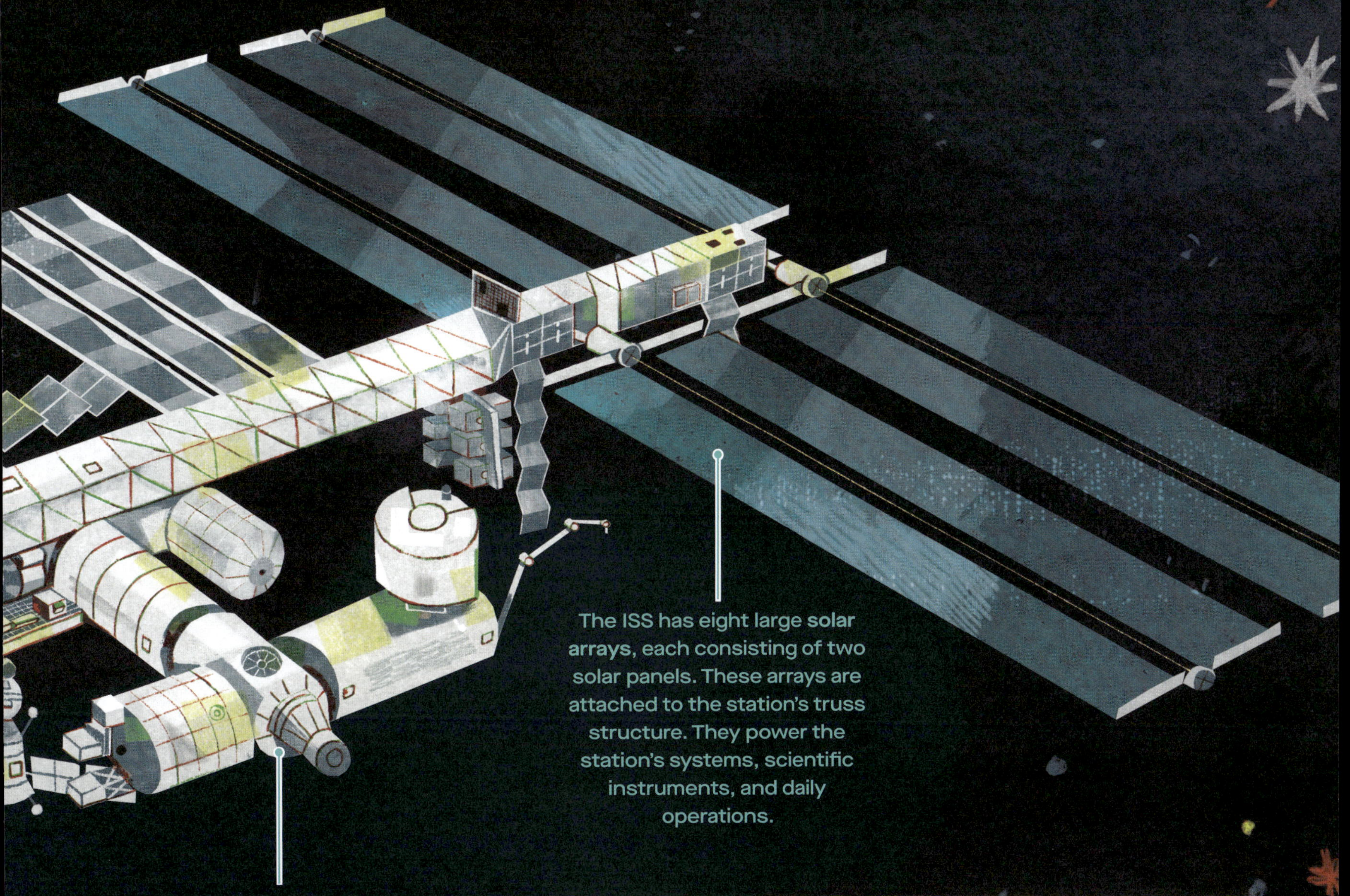

The ISS has eight large **solar arrays**, each consisting of two solar panels. These arrays are attached to the station's truss structure. They power the station's systems, scientific instruments, and daily operations.

Harmony is an American module with four small, cupboard-like spaces that are used as bedrooms.

Robotic arms are attached to the outside of the ISS. They were first used to build the spacecraft, but now are used for tasks such as operating experiments, or moving astronauts around when they are outside the ISS on spacewalks.

37

IN THE ISS

LOOK INSIDE

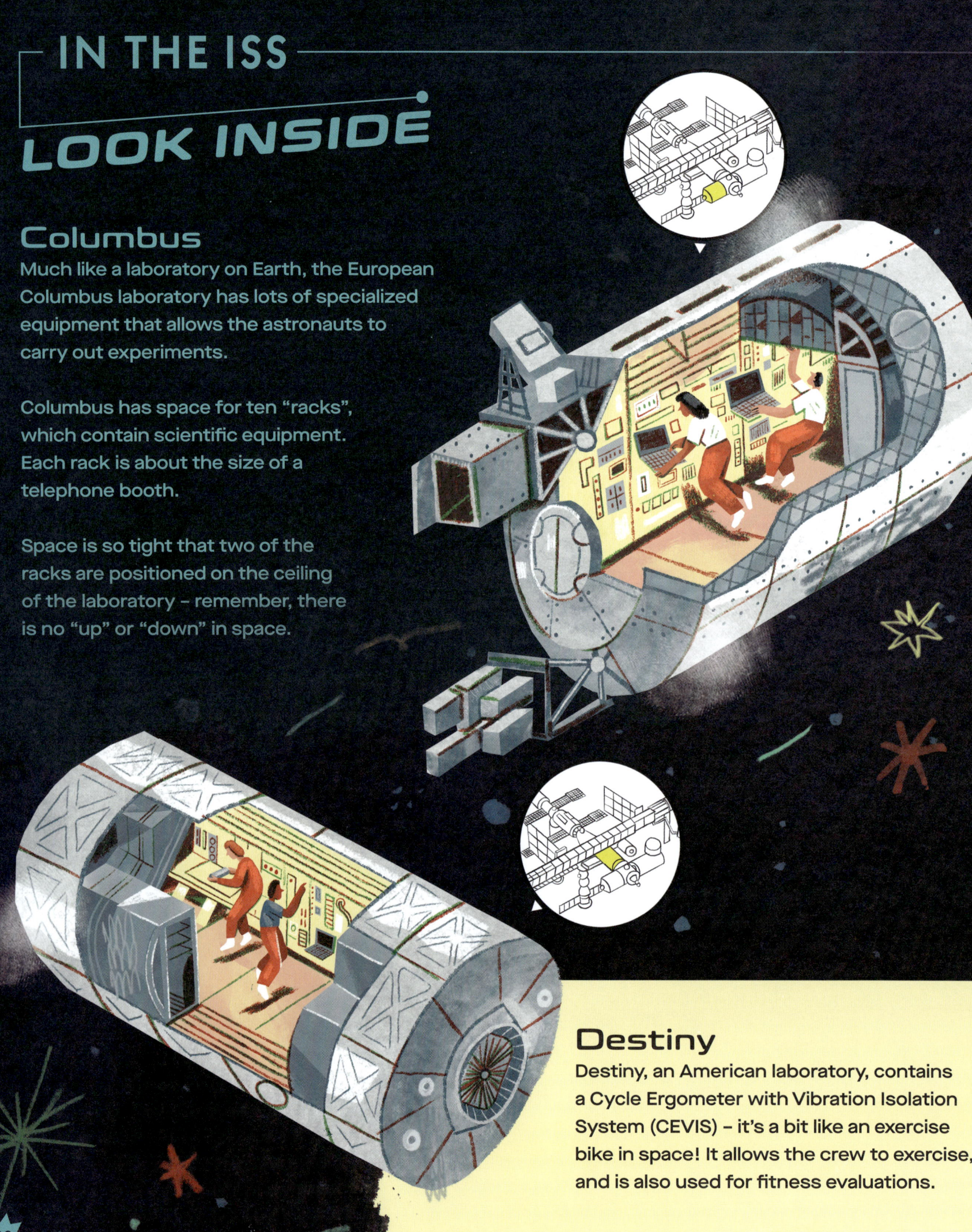

Columbus
Much like a laboratory on Earth, the European Columbus laboratory has lots of specialized equipment that allows the astronauts to carry out experiments.

Columbus has space for ten "racks", which contain scientific equipment. Each rack is about the size of a telephone booth.

Space is so tight that two of the racks are positioned on the ceiling of the laboratory – remember, there is no "up" or "down" in space.

Destiny
Destiny, an American laboratory, contains a Cycle Ergometer with Vibration Isolation System (CEVIS) – it's a bit like an exercise bike in space! It allows the crew to exercise, and is also used for fitness evaluations.

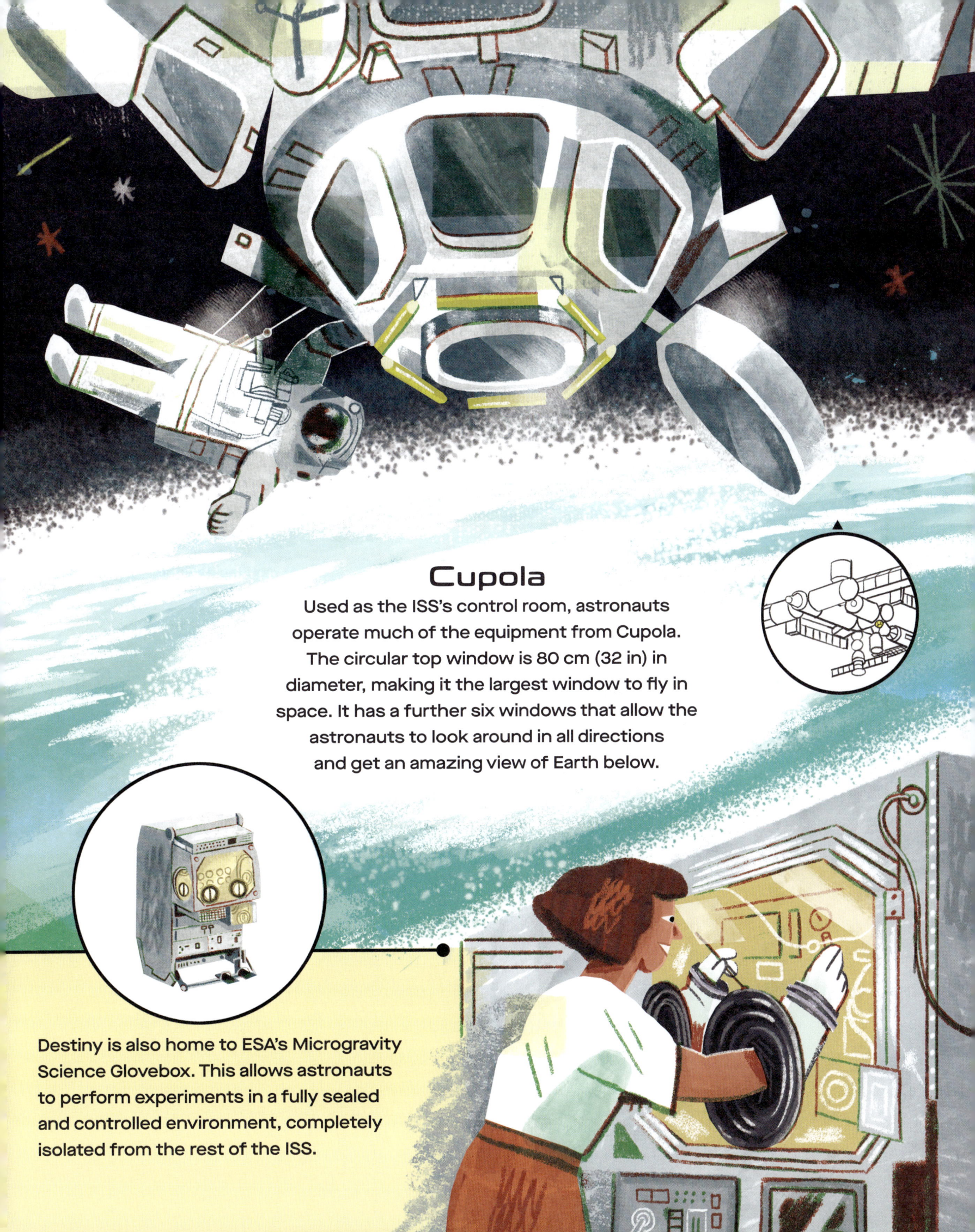

Cupola

Used as the ISS's control room, astronauts operate much of the equipment from Cupola. The circular top window is 80 cm (32 in) in diameter, making it the largest window to fly in space. It has a further six windows that allow the astronauts to look around in all directions and get an amazing view of Earth below.

Destiny is also home to ESA's Microgravity Science Glovebox. This allows astronauts to perform experiments in a fully sealed and controlled environment, completely isolated from the rest of the ISS.

LIFE AS AN ASTRONAUT

An **astronaut** is someone who serves as a crew member during a spaceflight. Astronauts perform duties related to space exploration, but they also have to undertake everyday tasks while experiencing "weightlessness".

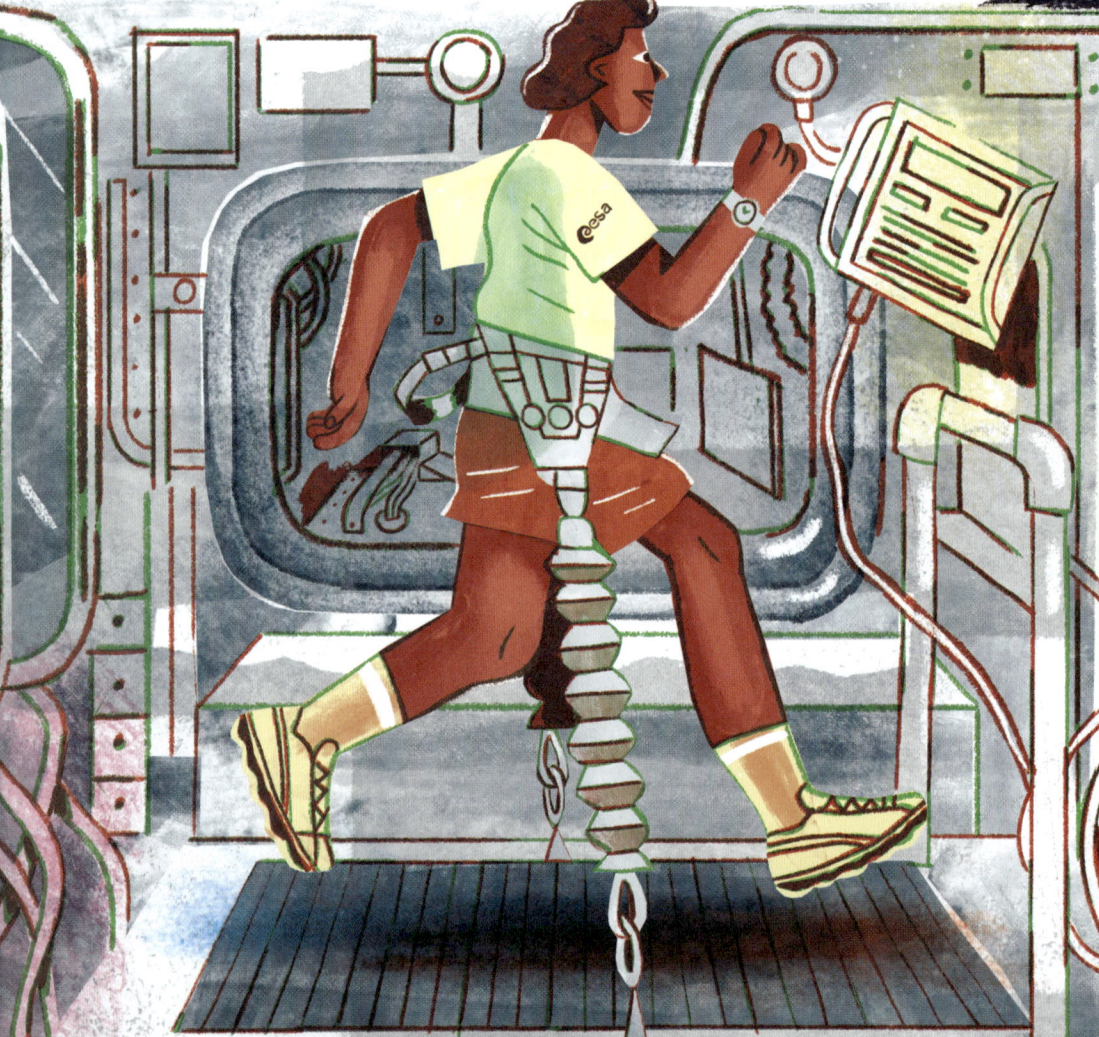

Space days
After a quick clean with a soapy cloth, the crew have breakfast and go through their jobs for the day with mission control. Astronauts have three meals per day, along with snacks and drinks. It is important that they keep healthy, so at least two hours per day is spent on physical exercise.

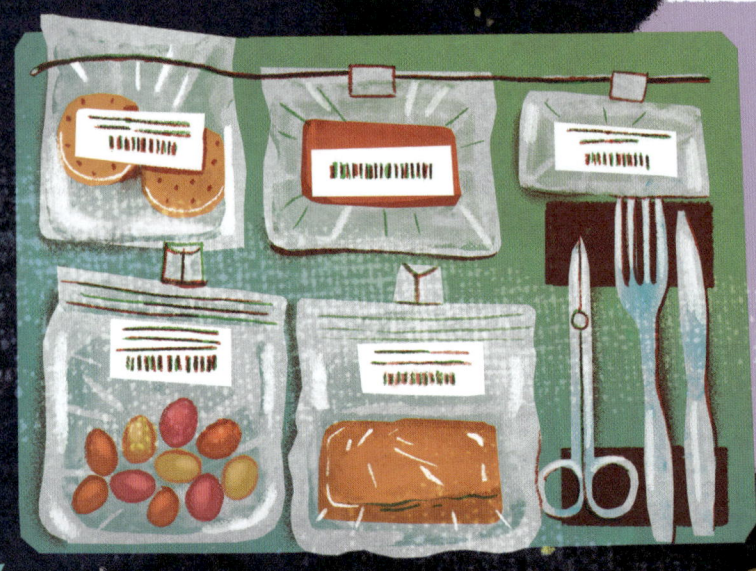

Space food
Most food eaten in space comes in cans or pouches. Resupply missions deliver fresh fruit, vegetables, and tortillas, but they need to be eaten soon after delivery to prevent them going bad. Tortillas are especially popular on the ISS because they don't produce crumbs like bread, which can cause problems in very weak gravity.

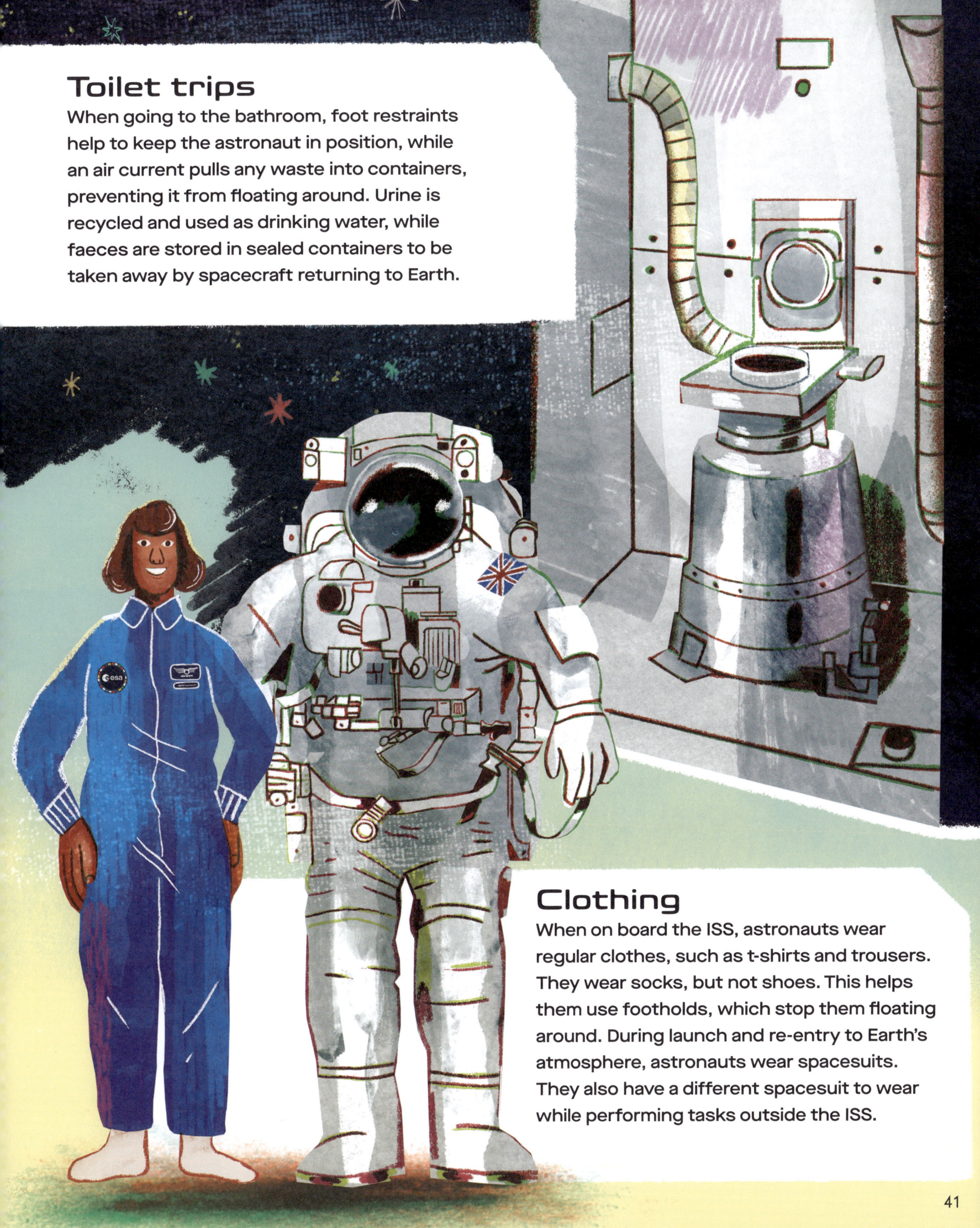

Toilet trips

When going to the bathroom, foot restraints help to keep the astronaut in position, while an air current pulls any waste into containers, preventing it from floating around. Urine is recycled and used as drinking water, while faeces are stored in sealed containers to be taken away by spacecraft returning to Earth.

Clothing

When on board the ISS, astronauts wear regular clothes, such as t-shirts and trousers. They wear socks, but not shoes. This helps them use footholds, which stop them floating around. During launch and re-entry to Earth's atmosphere, astronauts wear spacesuits. They also have a different spacesuit to wear while performing tasks outside the ISS.

THE LUNAR GATEWAY

The International Space Station orbits Earth, whereas the **Lunar Gateway** will orbit the Moon. This increased distance from Earth will mean the Gateway can provide support for future missions on the Moon, including the Artemis programme and potentially a manned mission to Mars.

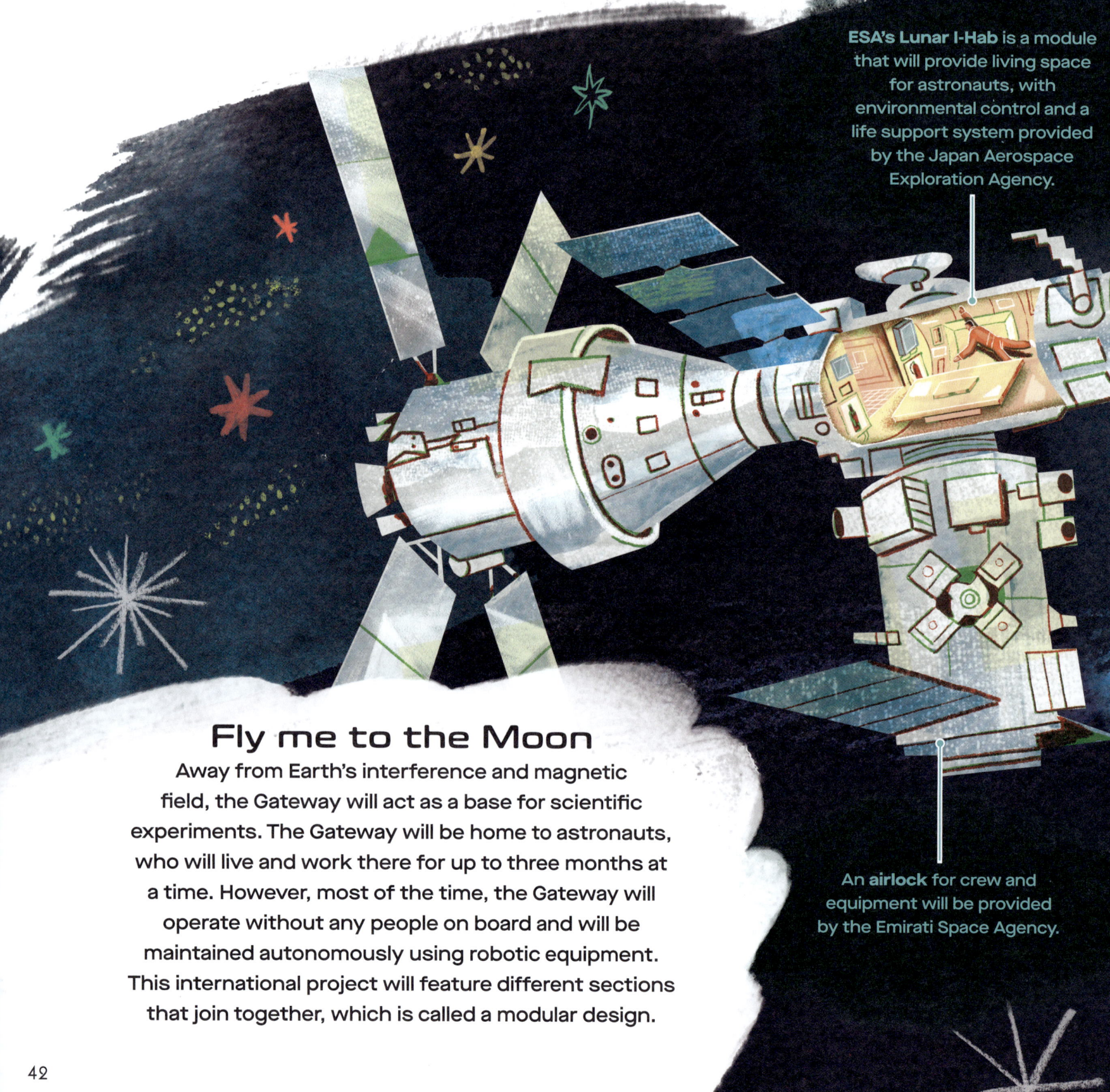

ESA's Lunar I-Hab is a module that will provide living space for astronauts, with environmental control and a life support system provided by the Japan Aerospace Exploration Agency.

An **airlock** for crew and equipment will be provided by the Emirati Space Agency.

Fly me to the Moon

Away from Earth's interference and magnetic field, the Gateway will act as a base for scientific experiments. The Gateway will be home to astronauts, who will live and work there for up to three months at a time. However, most of the time, the Gateway will operate without any people on board and will be maintained autonomously using robotic equipment. This international project will feature different sections that join together, which is called a modular design.

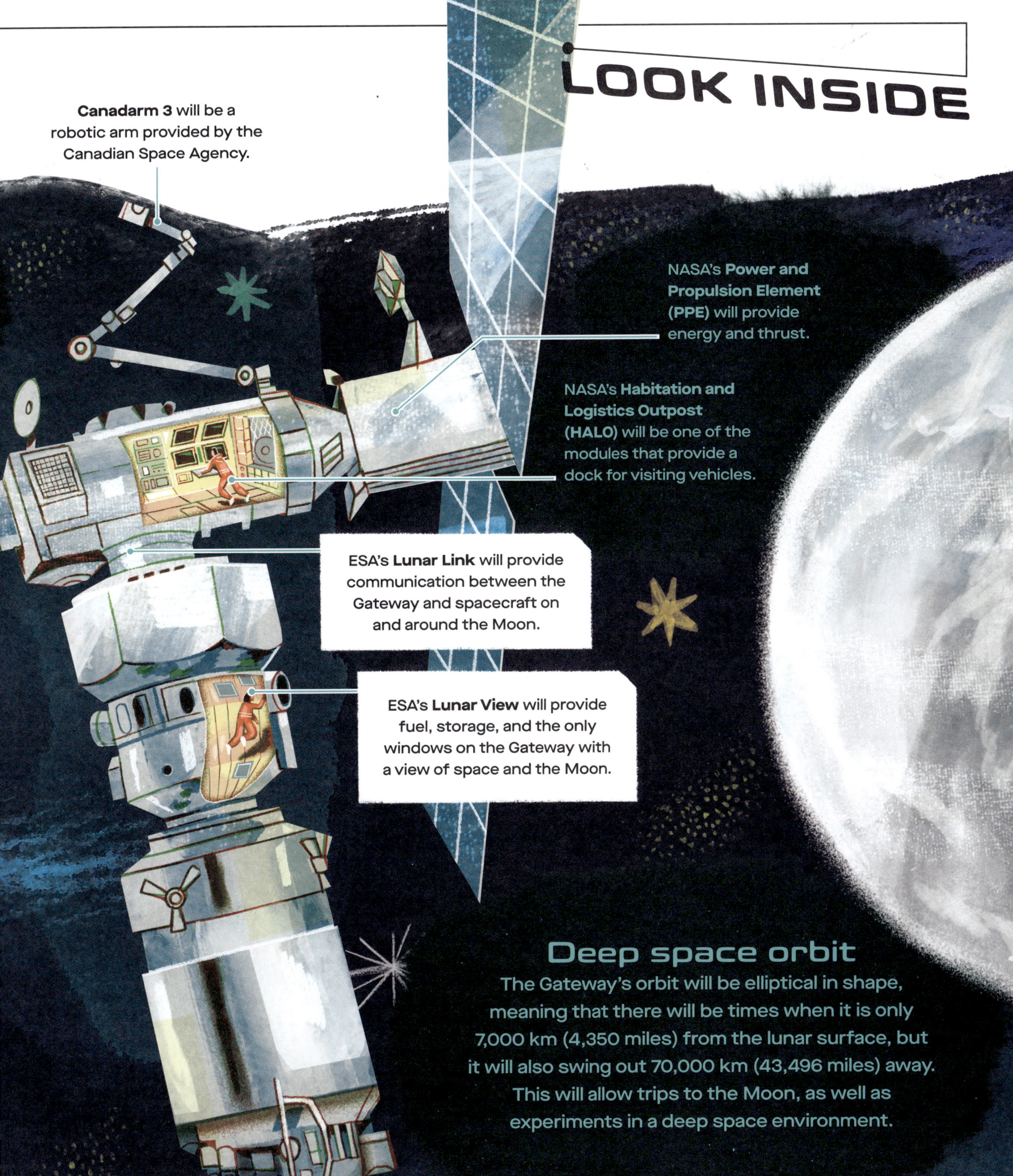

LOOK INSIDE

Canadarm 3 will be a robotic arm provided by the Canadian Space Agency.

NASA's **Power and Propulsion Element (PPE)** will provide energy and thrust.

NASA's **Habitation and Logistics Outpost (HALO)** will be one of the modules that provide a dock for visiting vehicles.

ESA's **Lunar Link** will provide communication between the Gateway and spacecraft on and around the Moon.

ESA's **Lunar View** will provide fuel, storage, and the only windows on the Gateway with a view of space and the Moon.

Deep space orbit

The Gateway's orbit will be elliptical in shape, meaning that there will be times when it is only 7,000 km (4,350 miles) from the lunar surface, but it will also swing out 70,000 km (43,496 miles) away. This will allow trips to the Moon, as well as experiments in a deep space environment.

OTHER SPACECRAFT

As well as satellites and space stations, some of the most important and impressive spacecraft are those that have been on missions to explore the furthest reaches of the Solar System – from moons to planets, and asteroids to comets.

A LOOK AT LAUNCH VEHICLES

Launch vehicles are crucial for deploying satellites, probes, and other spacecraft into space, allowing for a wide range of scientific, commercial, and exploratory missions. They travel to an altitude of around 150 km (93 miles), for testing or suborbital missions, or higher to place payloads into space.

Ariane 6

Ariane 6 is Europe's new launcher. It will be capable of a wide range of missions, with the ability to carry both light and heavy payloads, allowing it to take part in missions such as Earth observation, telecommunications, meteorology, science, and navigation.

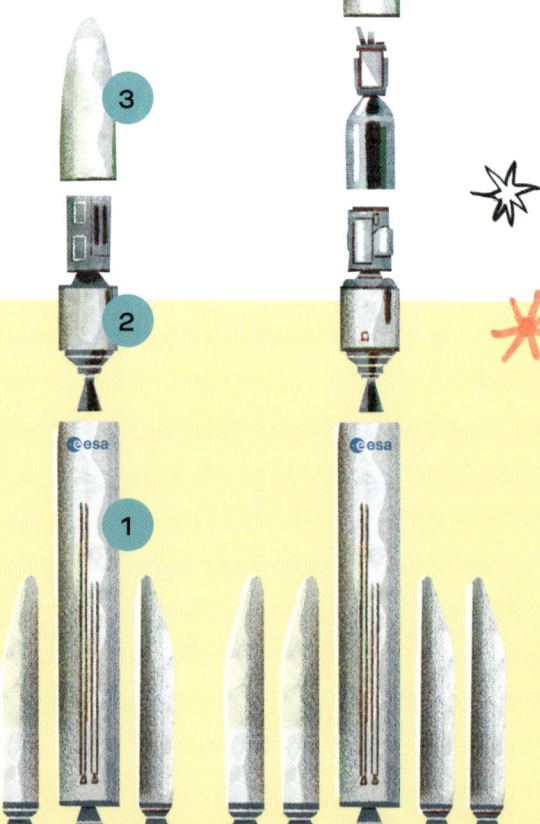

Ariane 6 is made of three parts, known as stages: the main stage (1) with two or four boosters; the upper stage (2); and the payload fairing (the nose cone) (3).

———

1. The **main stage,** also called the core stage, has **solid rocket boosters** to propel the Ariane 6 into flight.

———

2. The **upper stage** allows Ariane 6 to place one or more satellites into different orbits around the Earth by shutting down and restarting its engine. This means it can place each satellite where it needs to be.

Ariane 6 rockets stand at over 60 m (197 ft) tall – that's taller than 15 elephants stacked on top of one another.

LOOK INSIDE

3. The **fairing** is a carbon fibre-reinforced polymer composite nose cone that splits in two vertically. The fairing protects satellites from the thermal, acoustic, and aerodynamic stresses on the journey to space.

Space Launch System

NASA's Space Launch System (SLS) is so powerful that it can send NASA's Orion spacecraft, four astronauts, and large cargo directly to the Moon on a single mission. SLS will play a key role in the Artemis programme.

MOON EXPLORATION

The Lunar Roving Vehicle

Often called the Moon Buggy, the Lunar Roving Vehicle (LRV) was a battery-powered, four-wheeled rover used on the Moon in the Apollo 15, 16, and 17 missions during 1971 and 1972. It could carry two astronauts, equipment, and cargo, such as lunar samples.

A television camera transmitted footage directly to Earth.

The control console featured many switches and dials, which displayed various pieces of information.

A toolbox was filled with equipment.

The Lunar Communications Relay Unit provided image transmission to Earth via an antenna.

Batteries (located between the front wheels) provided power to the LRV. They were non-rechargeable.

The control stick was situated between the two seats, which controlled the four drive motors, two steering motors, and brakes.

Wire-mesh tyres with titanium braces provided traction on the lunar surface.

Argonaut

Europe's autonomous lunar lander, Argonaut, is being designed to take part in various missions, with many options for its payloads. It is planned that Argonaut will be able to deliver cargo, infrastructure, scientific equipment, lunar rovers, and even a power station to the Moon's surface. Launched via an Ariane 6 rocket, Argonaut could get to the Moon in a week. It will have the ability to land on any part of the lunar surface.

The Lunar Descent Element (LDE) will be responsible for flying to the Moon and landing on target.

The Cargo Platform Element (CPE) is the interface between the lander and its payload, and will include the power, thermal, communication and data handling systems.

The payload will contain the various cargo for astronauts near the landing site, a rover, technology demonstration packages, production facilities using resources on the Moon, a lunar telescope, or even a power station.

COMETS AND ASTEROIDS

While **comets** are made of ice, dust, and rocky material, **asteroids** are made up of rocky material and metals.

Comets are important because scientists believe that they could contain the elements that kick-start life on planets. Scientists study asteroids to learn about the Solar System's history, and to ensure they are not a threat to Earth.

Giotto

Giotto was launched in 1985 and was Europe's first mission into deep space.

It photographed Halley's Comet and provided the first close-up images of the central solid part of a comet, called the nucleus.

On top of the spacecraft was a 1.5 m (5 ft) dish antenna, which continually pointed towards Earth during its encounter with the comet to ensure non-stop communications.

Rosetta

Launched in 2004, Rosetta's mission was to visit Comet 67P/Churyumov–Gerasimenko and study its nucleus and environment.

This ESA mission carried 11 scientific instruments on one side of the spacecraft. It also carried a 100 kg (220 lb) lander called Philae, designed to be landed on the actual comet.

LOOK INSIDE

Hera

Hera, launched in October 2024, is a planetary defence mission. It will collect valuable data about an asteroid, Didymos, and its moonlet, Dimorphos. In particular, Hera will help scientists better understand the structure of Dimorphos and how it was altered by NASA's DART mission, which deliberately crashed into the asteroid in 2022 in the first test of asteroid deflection.

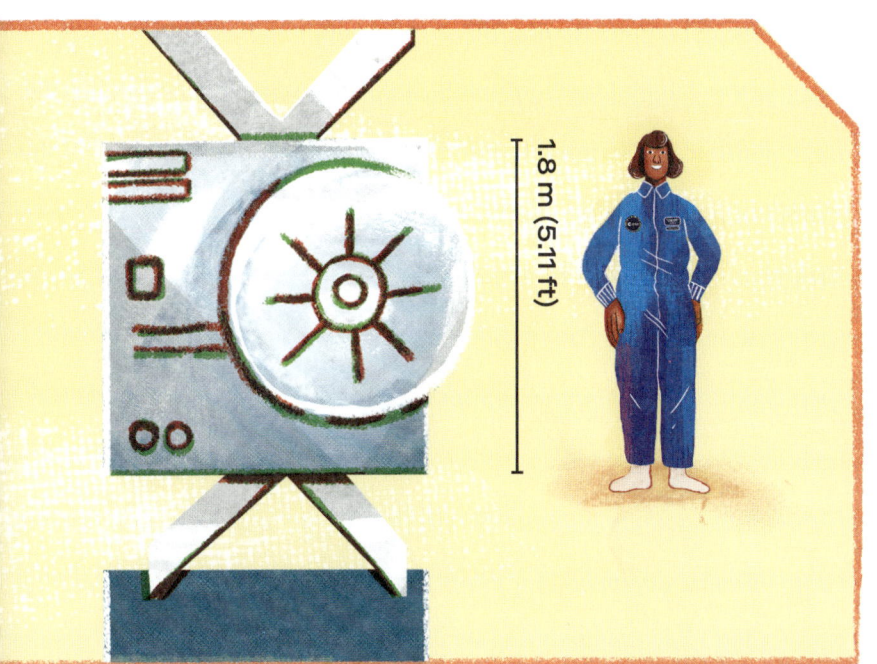

1.8 m (5.11 ft)

A pair of **cameras** will study the crater left by DART.

The **Thermal Infrared Imager** will help provide a detailed image of the asteroid.

HyperScout is an imager that observes its targets in more colours than the human eye can see.

Hera will release two Cubesats – a type of mini satellite – to study Didymos. They are called **Juventas and Milani**.

STUDYING THE SUN

SOHO

The **Solar and Heliospheric Observatory (SOHO)** was launched in 1995 and is stationed 1.5 million km (930,000 miles) away from Earth. It keeps a constant watch on the Sun, sending pictures and data back to Earth.

SOHO looks at everything from the Sun's hot interior to its visible surface, and even its stormy atmosphere, where solar winds blow out to distant regions of our Solar System.

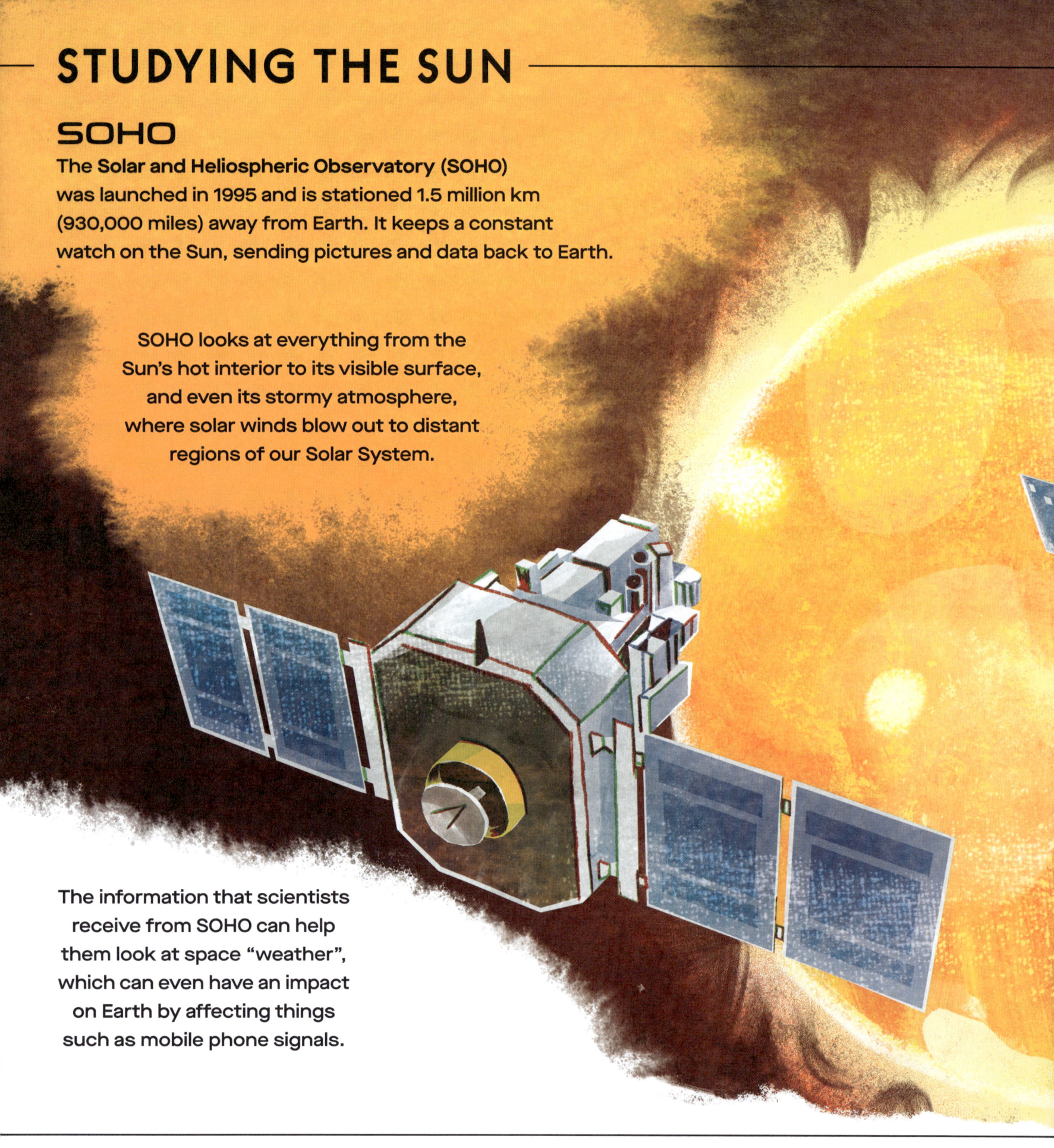

The information that scientists receive from SOHO can help them look at space "weather", which can even have an impact on Earth by affecting things such as mobile phone signals.

Why does the Sun have an 11-year cycle of rising and falling magnetic activity?

What heats up the upper layer of the Sun's atmosphere to millions of degrees Celsius?

LOOK INSIDE

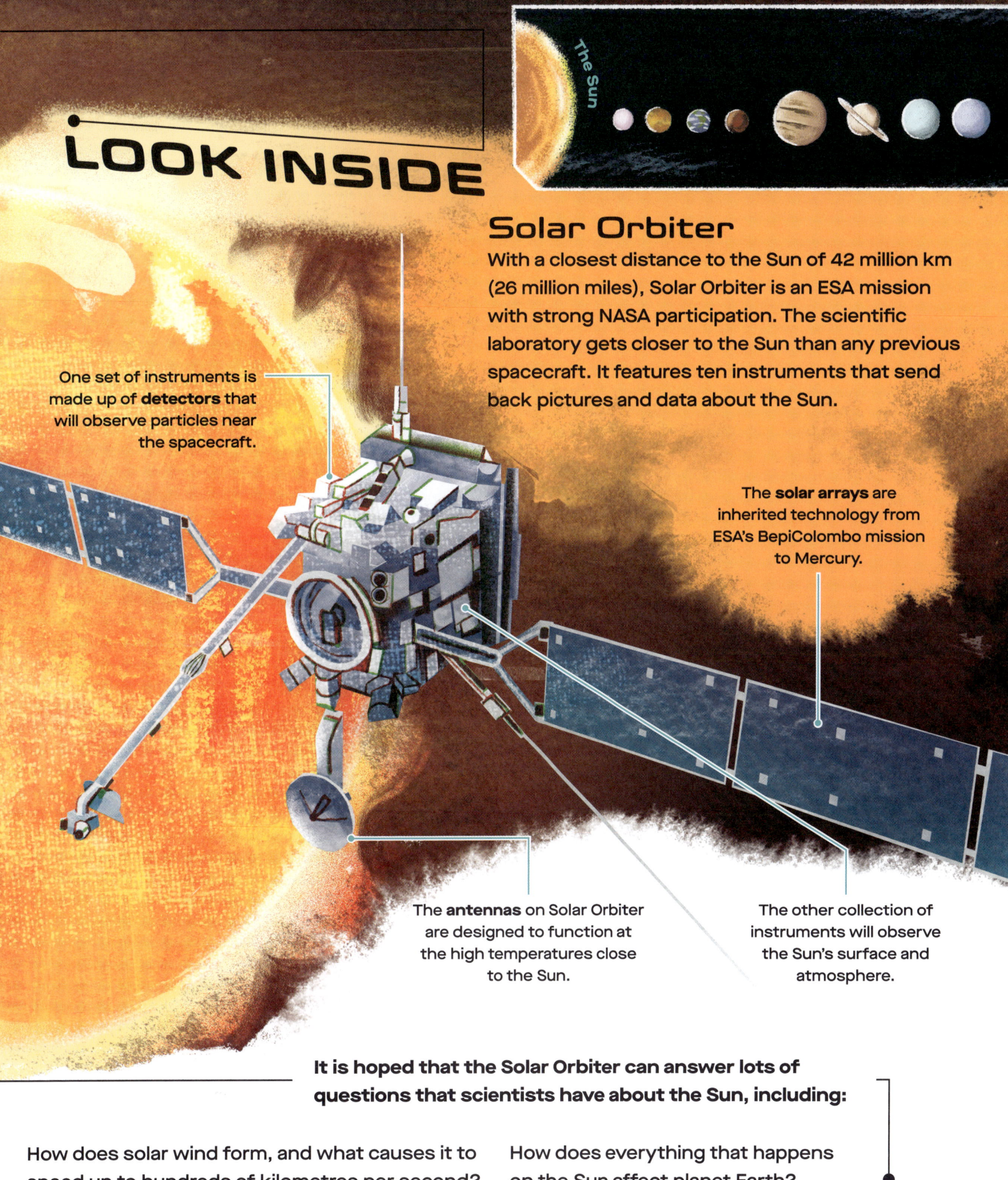

Solar Orbiter

With a closest distance to the Sun of 42 million km (26 million miles), Solar Orbiter is an ESA mission with strong NASA participation. The scientific laboratory gets closer to the Sun than any previous spacecraft. It features ten instruments that send back pictures and data about the Sun.

One set of instruments is made up of **detectors** that will observe particles near the spacecraft.

The **solar arrays** are inherited technology from ESA's BepiColombo mission to Mercury.

The **antennas** on Solar Orbiter are designed to function at the high temperatures close to the Sun.

The other collection of instruments will observe the Sun's surface and atmosphere.

It is hoped that the Solar Orbiter can answer lots of questions that scientists have about the Sun, including:

How does solar wind form, and what causes it to speed up to hundreds of kilometres per second?

How does everything that happens on the Sun affect planet Earth?

THE SECRETS OF SATURN

The Cassini–Huygens mission launched in October 1997 as a joint endeavour of ESA, NASA, and ASI. It was made up of the Cassini orbiter and the Huygens probe. This huge, interplanetary spacecraft carried instruments designed to study Saturn, its rings, and its moons.

Cassini–Huygens took almost seven years to reach Saturn, travelling nearly 3.5 billion km (2.2 billion miles). As well as mapping the surface of Saturn's largest moon, Titan, with an imaging radar, it also studied the moon's orange clouds and nitrogen-rich atmosphere.

Huygens

On Christmas Day 2004, ESA's **Huygens** probe separated from Cassini. Three weeks later it entered Titan's thick atmosphere and became the first probe to reach the surface of another planet's moon.

A heat shield protected Huygens as it got closer to Titan, and then a parachute helped to slow its descent. It eventually landed on a dry riverbed covered in small, icy boulders.

LOOK INSIDE

Saturn

Cassini

Huygens used its six instruments to send data back to Cassini, which then relayed it to Earth.

Cassini discovered geysers of ice and organic molecules at the south pole of Enceladus, another of Saturn's moons. It is thought that this could indicate that Enceladus has an underground ocean, with a possible environment for life.

As well as sending back data about Saturn and its moons, the Cassini orbiter carried a DVD containing more than 616,400 signatures from the citizens of 81 countries, collected during a communication campaign.

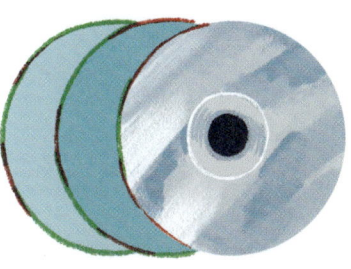

MISSION TO MARS

Mars Express is a space exploration mission that has been studying the planet Mars for more than 20 years.

Launched in June 2003, Mars Express was ESA's first planetary mission, with the aim of studying the Martian atmosphere and climates, the planet's structure, its mineralogy and its geology, and to search for traces of water.

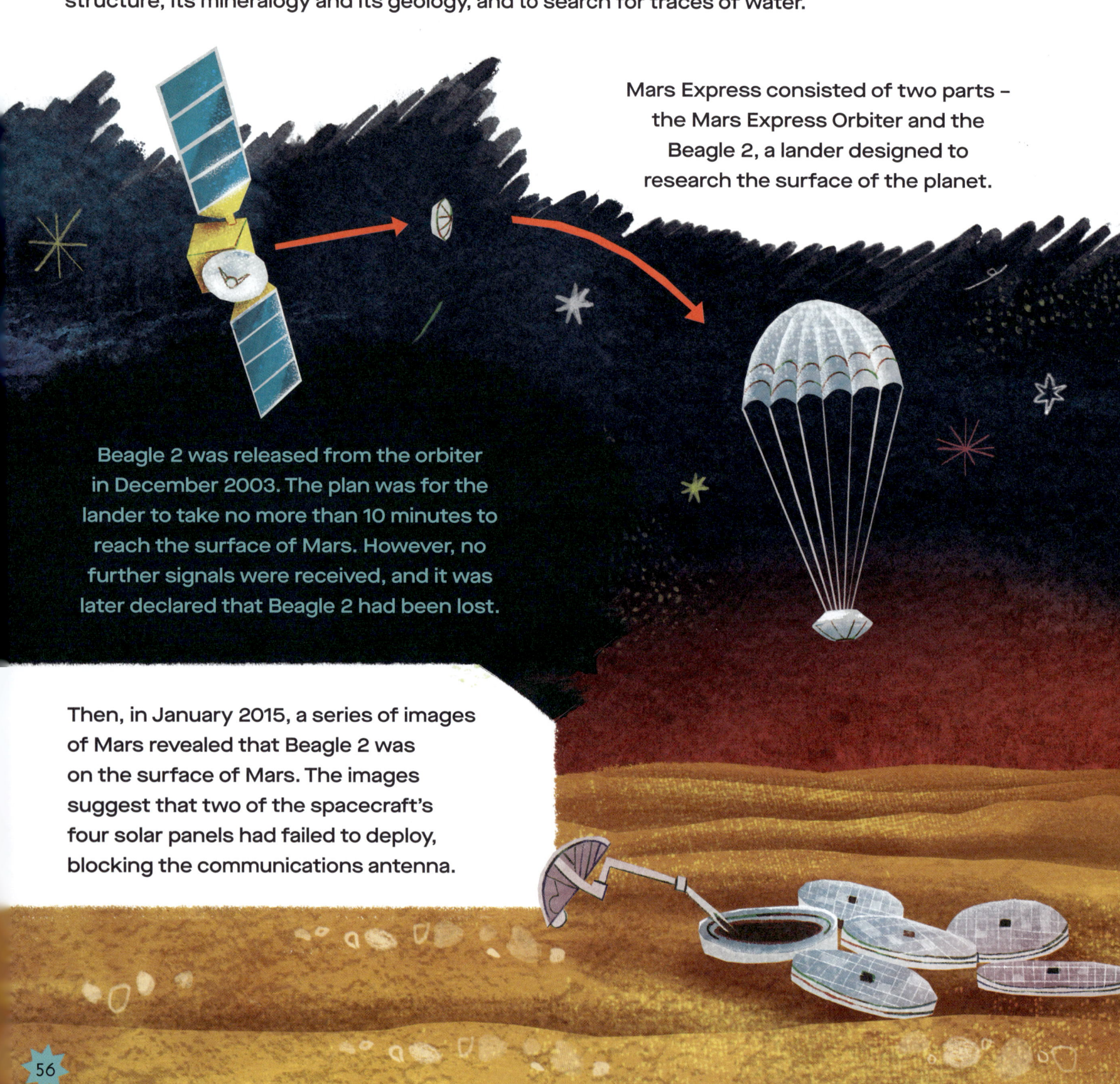

Mars Express consisted of two parts – the Mars Express Orbiter and the Beagle 2, a lander designed to research the surface of the planet.

Beagle 2 was released from the orbiter in December 2003. The plan was for the lander to take no more than 10 minutes to reach the surface of Mars. However, no further signals were received, and it was later declared that Beagle 2 had been lost.

Then, in January 2015, a series of images of Mars revealed that Beagle 2 was on the surface of Mars. The images suggest that two of the spacecraft's four solar panels had failed to deploy, blocking the communications antenna.

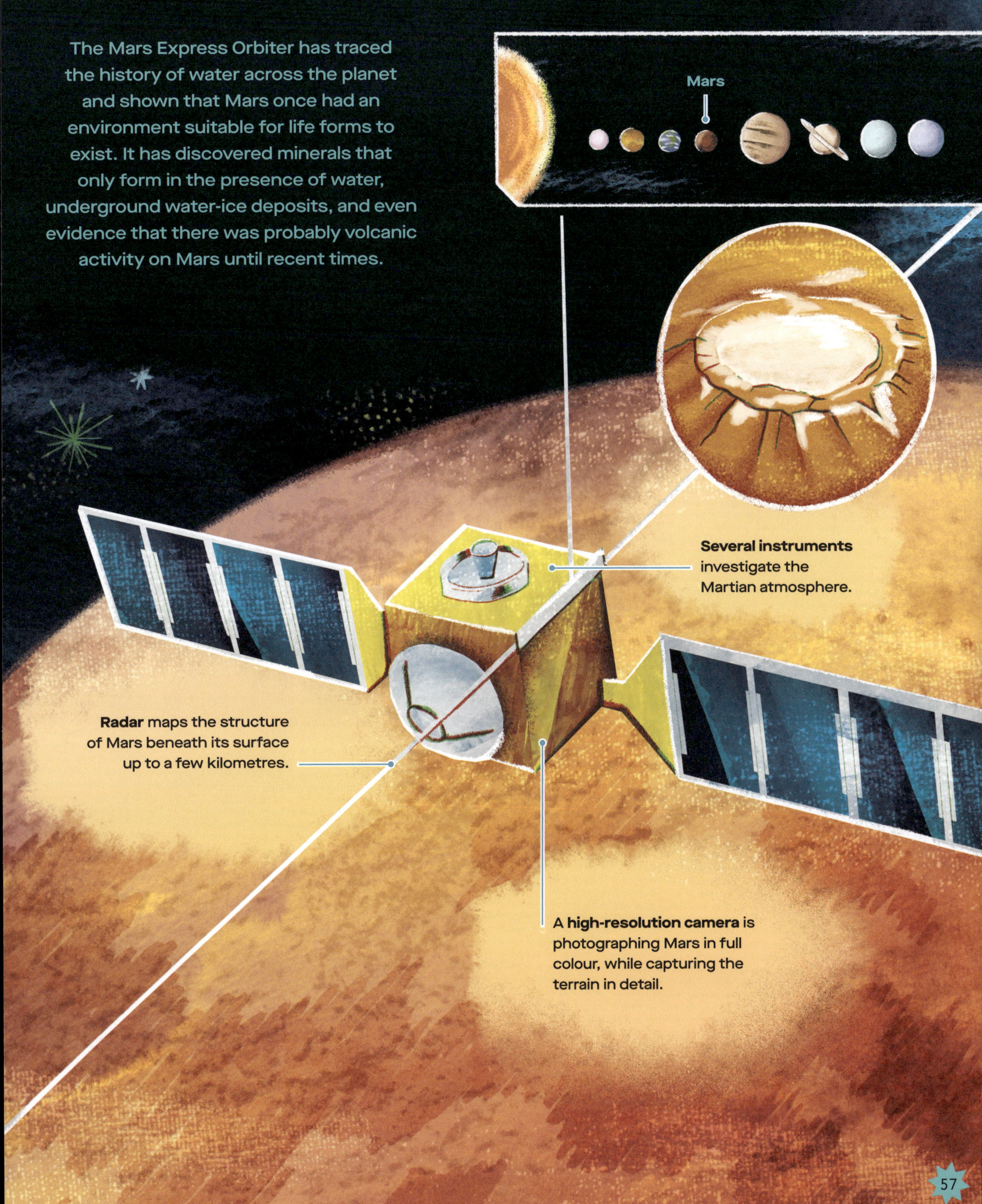

The Mars Express Orbiter has traced the history of water across the planet and shown that Mars once had an environment suitable for life forms to exist. It has discovered minerals that only form in the presence of water, underground water-ice deposits, and even evidence that there was probably volcanic activity on Mars until recent times.

Mars

Several instruments investigate the Martian atmosphere.

Radar maps the structure of Mars beneath its surface up to a few kilometres.

A **high-resolution camera** is photographing Mars in full colour, while capturing the terrain in detail.

57

VENTURING TO VENUS

Venus Express looks a lot like Mars Express, and that's because to save time and money it was built around the same design. It even used many of the spare instruments developed for the Mars Express and Rosetta missions.

Launched in 2005, Venus Express's mission was to study how Venus's atmosphere interacted with the planet's surface. It also looked at how its atmosphere and clouds were affected by solar winds and what impact this had on the evolution of the planet.

The environment of Venus is much hotter than that of Mars, which meant that some changes had to be made when the original Mars Express design was adapted to become the Venus Express. This ensured that the instruments could operate at the higher temperatures they would experience.

However, with Venus being closer to the Sun compared to Mars, it meant that there was increased solar radiation, allowing Venus Express's solar arrays to only be about half the size of those on Mars Express.

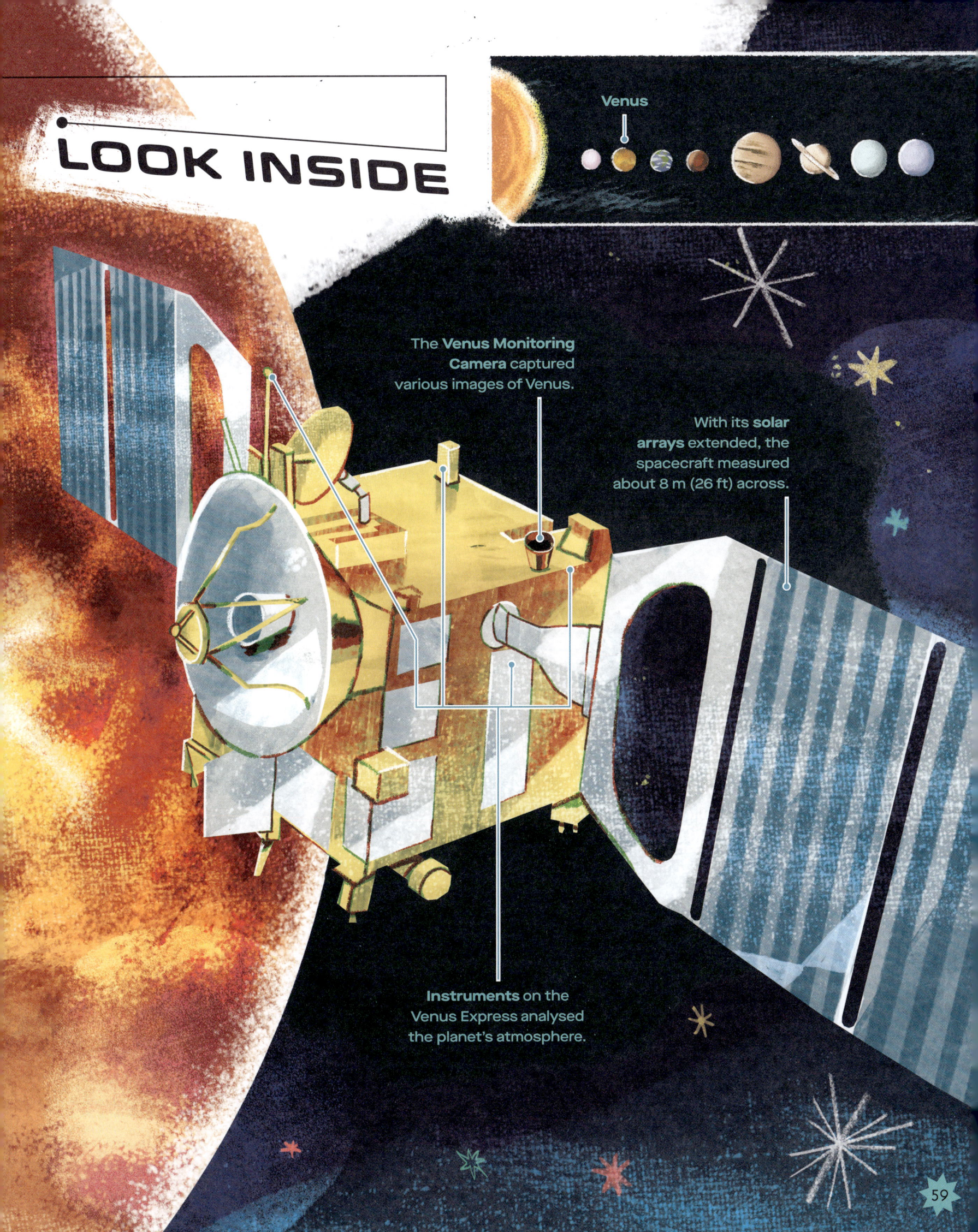
LOOK INSIDE

Venus

The **Venus Monitoring Camera** captured various images of Venus.

With its **solar arrays** extended, the spacecraft measured about 8 m (26 ft) across.

Instruments on the Venus Express analysed the planet's atmosphere.

THE MYSTERY OF MERCURY

BepiColombo is a joint European–Japanese mission to Mercury to study the planet's structure, atmosphere, and history.

Launched in 2018, it is due to arrive at Mercury in late 2026, with scientific operation scheduled to begin in early 2027. It will be the first mission to Mercury comprised of two spacecraft travelling together.

ESA's Mercury Planetary Orbiter (MPO) will study the planet's surface and interior.

Mercury is a small, desert-like world, and the least-explored planet in the Solar System. It is hoped that the BepiColombo mission will answer questions such as:

Why is there ice on the polar craters of the scorched planet?

A few months before going into Mercury's orbit, BepiColombo will release, or jettison, the spacecraft's transfer module, leaving the two connected orbiters to be captured by Mercury's gravity.

Mercury

JAXA's Mercury Magnetospheric Orbiter (MMO) will study the planet's magnetic field.

Once in Mercury's gravitational orbit, MPO and MIO will separate and observe Mercury in collaboration for an initial period of one year.

Why does Mercury have a magnetic field?

What are the mysterious "hollows" that have been seen on the surface?

61

JUICE TO JUPITER

The **Jupiter Icy Moons Explorer,** known as Juice, was launched by ESA in April 2023, and is due to arrive at its destination eight years later, in July 2031. Its mission is to make detailed observations of the giant gas planet and its three large, ocean-bearing moons – Ganymede, Callisto, and Europa.

Juice carries 10 scientific instruments that will analyse Jupiter's moons and their ability to host life. The mission will also discover details about Jupiter's weather and climate patterns.

The **Particle Environment Package** is made up of a package of sensors to identify the plasma environment of the Jupiter system and the icy moons.

The **geophysical package** is made up of instruments to investigate the moons' surfaces as well as Jupiter's atmosphere.

Juice is fitted with special **radiation shields** to help protect the special scientific equipment from Jupiter's powerful magnetic field.

Super solar-powered

Jupiter is five times farther from the Sun than Earth, so Juice gets much less sunlight than satellites orbiting our planet. To generate enough electricity, Juice is fitted with enormous cross-shaped solar panels, measuring 85 m² (915 ft²).

The **in situ package** of instruments will study the surrounding magnetic and electric fields of Jupiter and its satellites.

Underground oceans

Scientists are hoping to confirm the existence of underground oceans beneath the icy crust of Ganymede, Jupiter's largest moon. It was the Galileo mission that first spotted odd disturbances in the magnetic field around Jupiter. Scientists think that these are caused by salty oceans below the surface of Ganymede.

TELESCOPES

A space telescope, also known as a space observatory, is a telescope in outer space used to observe astronomical objects. They are useful because they allow scientists to view objects and places without the interference of light pollution from Earth, clouds, or other atmospheric conditions.

HUMUNGOUS HERSCHEL
LOOK INSIDE

The **Herschel Space Observatory** launched in May 2009. Herschel's mission was to study interesting objects in our Solar System and across the Universe, focusing on the formation and evolution of stars and galaxies.

The instruments on board were able to help astronomers work out where new stars were forming and to study the action in detail.

The **sun shade** protected the telescope from unwanted sources of light and heat.

The telescope used two **mirrors** to capture light.

Two **cameras** captured images across different types of light, while another instrument searched for different chemicals across the Universe.

The **solar array** converted sunlight into electrical energy.

These instruments had to be cooled to a temperature of −273.15°C (−459.67°F), close to absolute zero, using a state-of-the-art cryogenic system. This allowed Herschel to make highly sensitive observations in the cold Universe.

The **service module** was responsible for controlling the spacecraft's important functions.

The observatory was 7.5 m (25 ft) high and 4 m (13 ft) wide, with a launch mass of 3,400 kg (3.7 tons) – about the same as a pick-up truck.

It had the largest telescope ever flown into space, with a main mirror measuring 3.5 m (11 ft) across.

Herschel studied the "cold" Universe. It was able to see through dust clouds, and study star-forming regions and galactic centres, as well as search out hidden stars and unknown planets. It was also able to discover distant galaxies and find out how they formed, billions of years ago. The mission only ended in 2013 when the helium used to cool the instruments ran out.

MAPPING THE STARS

The James Webb Space Telescope

The largest, most powerful space telescope ever built, the James Webb Space Telescope (the Webb Telescope) stands as tall as a three-storey building and as long as a tennis court. The Webb Telescope is an international partnership between NASA, ESA, and CSA.

The Webb Telescope features **infrared cameras** that capture images through space dust, detecting heat radiation from objects that are hidden – similar to how night-vision goggles work.

The Webb Telescope's **mirror** is 6.5 m (21 ft) in diameter and is made up of 18 smaller, hexagonal mirrors. Each of these mirrors is coated in a thin layer of gold that helps to reflect infrared light.

The Webb Telescope was too big to fit in any rocket, so it had to be folded up. It was only once in space that it was unfolded. The unfolding took two weeks to complete.

The Webb Telescope launched in 2021 on an Ariane 5, from Europe's Spaceport in French Guiana. It orbits the Sun, 1.5 million kilometres (930,000 miles) from Earth.

The underside of the Webb Telescope includes a solar array, a communication antenna, and instruments for steering and control.

A **thermal tent** protects the spacecraft and payload from direct illumination by the Sun, and helps to provide a stable and low temperature environment.

LOOK INSIDE

A **sunshield** is deployed around the fixed solar array.

Gaia contains **optical telescopes** that work with three scientific instruments and a one-billion-pixel camera.

Gaia

Launched in 2013, Gaia was ESA's space observatory. Its mission was to create a precise 3D map of more than a thousand million stars throughout the Milky Way Galaxy and beyond. Not only this, it also recorded the way the stars move, how bright they are, their temperature, and what they are made of.

SEARCHING AMONG STARS

There are secrets among the stars, from **exoplanets** to **dark matter**.

Exoplanets are planets outside our Solar System. Even though almost 6,000 exoplanets have been confirmed, we know very little about them.

CHEOPS

CHEOPS is ESA's Characterising Exoplanet Satellite, with the mission to study bright, nearby stars that are already known to host exoplanets.

CHEOPS will work by measuring a planet's size as it passes in front of its host star. This information will help scientists understand these alien worlds.

CHEOPS features two titanium plaques with engravings of 2,748 children's drawings of space.

The payload is a telescope made up of a number of clever units. CHEOPS has revealed some amazing secrets, including a rugby ball-shaped exoplanet that has been stretched by gravitational forces.

In the dark

Scientists think that the things we can see, such as stars, planets, and gas clouds, only make up 5 per cent of the entire Universe. The rest is "stuff" that we can't detect.

Scientists believe that the other 95 per cent of the Universe is made up of something called "dark matter" (around 25 per cent) and "dark energy" (around 70 per cent). It is thought that dark matter, dark energy, and gravity have all played a part in how our Universe has developed.

Euclid

Euclid is an ESA spacecraft, launched in 2023, carrying a wide-angle telescope with the mission to discover more about the expansion of the Universe in distant dark space and whether we fully understand gravity. It's a fascinating mission that could provide significant insights into some of the biggest mysteries in cosmology.

The 1.2-m (4-ft)-diameter **mirror telescope** is insulated to protect it from temperature changes.

A camera collects visible light. It takes very sharp images of galaxies over a much larger fraction of sky than would be possible from the ground.

A near-infrared camera is dedicated to making measurements of galaxies, which involves determining how much light they emit. This is useful information to have when estimating the distance to each galaxy.

ESA MEMBER STATES

Member states

Country	Date of ratification
Sweden	April 1976
Switzerland	November 1976
Germany	July 1977
Denmark	September 1977
Italy	February 1978
United Kingdom	March 1978
Belgium	October 1978
Netherlands	February 1979
Spain	February 1979
France	October 1980
Ireland	December 1980
Austria	December 1986
Norway	December 1986
Finland	January 1995
Portugal	November 2000
Greece	March 2005
Luxembourg	June 2005
Czech Republic	August 2008
Romania	December 2011
Poland	November 2012
Estonia	September 2015
Hungary	November 2015
Slovenia	January 2025

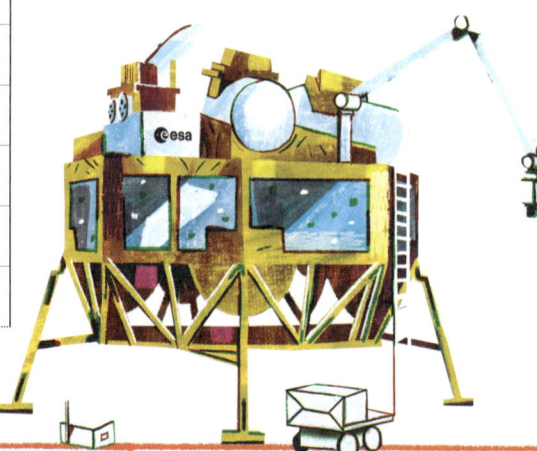

Associate members

Country	Date of agreement
Latvia	July 2020
Lithuania	May 2021
Slovak Republic	October 2022

Cooperating state

Country	Date of agreement
Canada	January 1979

States with cooperation agreements

Country	Date of agreement
Bulgaria	April 2015
Cyprus	July 2016
Croatia	February 2023
Malta	September 2024

GLOSSARY

A

Altitude – The height of an object above Earth's surface.

Antenna – A device used to send or receive signals.

Asteroid – A small, rocky celestial body that orbits the Sun.

Atmosphere – The layer of gases surrounding a planet.

C

Canadian Space Agency (CSA) – Canada's national space agency.

Comet – An icy celestial body that orbits the Sun.

Cryogenics – The study of materials and systems at extremely low temperatures, usually below −150°C (−238°F).

CubeSat – A square-shaped, tiny satellite. CubeSats can be stacked together to be part of or create a larger spacecraft.

E

European Commission (EC) – The European Union's (EU) executive branch, meaning it is responsible for proposing EU laws, managing EU budgets, and implementing EU policies.

European Union (EU) – A political and economic union of 27 European countries.

Exoplanet – A planet located beyond our Solar System, orbiting a star other than the Sun.

F

Fairing – A structural part of a launch vehicle that forms the nose cone, used to protect payload (such as a satellite) during launch.

G

Gravity – A force that pulls all things with mass or energy towards each other.

Gyroscope – A device used for measuring or maintaining the rotation of an object.

I

Interplanetary – Existing between, or the journey between, planets.

J

Japan Aerospace Exploration Agency (JAXA) – Japan's national space agency.

L

Laboratory – A space equipped for scientific experiments and research.

Lander – A spacecraft designed to land on a planet or moon.

Launch vehicle – Rocket-powered spacecraft designed to carry payloads – such as satellites, scientific instruments, or crewed spacecraft – from Earth into space.

M

Magnetic field – A region of space around a magnet or moving electric charge where magnetic forces can be detected. Planets and other celestial bodies in space often generate a magnetic field within, which extends out into space.

Moonlet – A small moon.

N

National Aeronautics and Space Administration (NASA) – USA's national space agency.

Navigation – The process of determining and controlling the movement or position of a vehicle, person, or object from one place to another.

O

Orbit – A curved path that an object follows around another object.

Orbiter – A spacecraft designed to circle an object without landing.

Ozone – A gas made up of three oxygen atoms. It forms naturally in the upper atmosphere, but it can also be human-made.

P

Payload – A part of a spacecraft, launcher, or satellite that is intended to perform the space mission's primary function.

Planet – A celestial body that orbits a star, has enough mass for its gravity to pull it into a spherical shape, and has cleared its orbital path around a star of other objects.

Probe – An uncrewed spacecraft designed to travel beyond Earth's orbit to collect scientific data.

R

Radiation – Energy that moves from one place to another as a wave or particle.

Rover – A robotic vehicle used for exploring the surface of a planet or moon.

S

Satellite – An object that orbits around another object in space.

Service module – The part of a spacecraft that provides support systems for the crew or payload during a mission.

Solar array – A system of connected solar panels that generate electricity from sunlight.

Soviet Union – A former country (1922–1991) made up of Russia and other republics. It was officially known as the Union of Soviet Socialist Republics (USSR).

Space station – A large, artificial satellite that humans are able to live and work on.

Spacecraft – A vehicle that travels in space.

Suborbital mission – A spaceflight where a spacecraft reaches space but does not complete an orbit around Earth.

T

Thrust – The pushing force that moves a rocket (or any vehicle) forward.

V

Velocity – The speed of an object in a particular direction.

INDEX

A

agriculture 30
air 31
Albert II 10
altitude and orbit control system 21
amateur rockets 12
antennas 15, 20, 24, 25, 48, 50, 53, 56, 68
Apollo missions 11, 48
Arctic Weather Satellite (AWS) 31
Argonaut 49
Ariane 5 68
Ariane 6 16, 46, 49
Artemis programme 13, 42, 47
asteroids 12, 13, 50–51
astronauts 40–41
astronomy 10
atmosphere
    Earth 29
    Jupiter 62
    Mars 56–57
    Mercury 60
    solar 52
    temperature and humidity of 31
    Venus 58–59

B

batteries 24, 25
Beagle 2 (spacecraft) 56
BeiDou (BDS) 26
BepiColombo 13, 14–15, 53, 60–61

C

Callisto 62
cameras 15
    orbiters 51, 57, 59
    rovers 48
    telescopes 66, 68, 69, 71
carbon monoxide 29
Cassini-Huygens mission 12, 54–55
Chandrayaan-3 (spacecraft) 13
CHEOPS 70
climate change 31
climate observation satellites 30–31
clothing 41
clouds 31
Columbus module (ISS) 37, 38
Comet 67P/Churyumov-Gerasimenko 50
comets 11, 50
communication payloads 21
communication system 14, 15
computers (satellites) 20
Copernicus Sentinel-2A 13, 30
Cos-B 11, 25
cryogenics 66
CSXT GoFast 12
Cupola (ISS) 37, 39
Cycle Ergometer with Vibration Isolation System (CEVIS) 38

D

dark energy 71
dark matter 71
DART mission 51
deep space orbit 43
Destiny module (ISS) 37, 38–39
Didymos 13, 51
Dimorphos 13, 51
docking ports 36, 43
dust clouds 67

E

EarthCARE 31
Enceladus 55
engines 14
ESA member states 72-73
Euclid 71
Europa 62
exoplanets 70
experiments
    ISS 37, 38, 39
    Lunar Gateway 42
Explorer 1 (spacecraft) 10, 25

F

fairings 46, 47
fitness (astronauts) 38, 41
Flexible Combined Imager 28
food
    astronauts 40
    grown in space 13
fuel 17

G

Gagarin, Yuri 11
Gaia 12, 69
galaxies 66, 67, 71
Galilei, Galileo 10, 26
Galileo programme 26-27
Galileo space probe 11
gamma rays 25
Ganymede 62, 63
gas clouds 71
geostationary orbit 23
Giotto mission 11, 50
Global Navigation Satellite System (GNSS) 26
Global Positioning System (GPS) 26
GLONASS system 26
gravity
    and expansion of the Universe 71
    Earth 16
    Mercury 61
gyroscopes 21

H

Halley's Comet 11, 50
Harmony module (ISS) 37
heat/sun shields 15, 54, 69
Hera mission 13, 51
Hershel Space Laboratory 66-67
Huygens probe 12, 54-55

I

infrared radiation 31
Infrared Sounder 29
Integrated Truss Structure (ISS) 36
International Space Station (ISS) 11, 13, 19, 36-39
interplanetary spacecraft 9

J

James Webb Space Telescope 13, 68
Jupiter 11, 62-63
Jupiter Icy Moons Explorer (Juice) 62-63

L

landers 9, 15, 49, 56
launch vehicles 8, 46-47
Lightning Imager 29
Low Earth orbit (LEO) 17, 22
Luna 2 (spacecraft) 10
Lunar Gateway 42-43
Lunar Roving Vehicle (LRV) 48

INDEX continued

M
magnetic fields
    Earth 42
    Jupiter 62, 63
    Mercury 61
Mars 11, 42, 56-57
Mars 3 (spacecraft) 11
Mars Express 56-57, 58
Medium Earth Orbit 22
Mercury 13, 15, 53, 60-61
Mercury Magnetospheric Orbiter (MIO) 15, 61
Mercury Planetary Orbiter (MPO) 60
Meteosat 11, 28-29
Microgravity Science Glovebox 39
Milky Way 69
Mir 35
mirrors (telescopes) 66, 68, 71
Moon
    exploration 48-49
    landings 10, 11, 13, 48, 49
    Lunar Gateway 42-43
    Space Launch System 47
moons 19
    Jupiter 62-63
    Saturn 54-55

N
natural disasters 30
navigation systems 22, 26-27
NEAR Shoemaker 12

O
oceans, Jupiter's underground 63
orbiters 9, 56-61
orbits
    Lunar Gateway 43
    satellites 22-23
Orion spacecraft 47
ozone 29

P
payload modules 14, 15, 46
planetary defence missions 51
polar-orbiting satellites 31

R
radiation shields 69
robotic arms 37, 43
rockets/launchers 16-17, 46-47
Rosetta mission 50, 58
rovers 9, 48, 49

S
Salyut 1 (space station) 11, 34
satellites 8, 10, 11, 18-31
    climate observation 30-31
    early 24-25
    Galileo programme 26-27
    orbits 22-23
    weather 11, 19, 28-29
Saturn 12, 54-55
search and rescue 26, 27
Skylab 34
SOHO (Solar and Heliospheric Observatory) 52-53
Solar Orbiter 13, 53
solar panels/arrays 14, 15, 21, 36, 53, 58, 59, 63, 68
solar radiation 31, 58

Solar System 11, 19, 50, 52, 66
solar wind 52, 53, 58
space capsules 8
space dust 67, 68
Space Launch System (SLS) 47
space observatories 12, 52-53, 65
space probes 9, 12, 13, 54
space shuttles 8
space stations 8, 11, 13, 32-43
    early 34-35
space telescopes 9, 64-71
spacecraft 8-9
    anatomy 14-15
spacecraft bus 20
spacesuits 41
spacewalks 37
SpaceX Dragon 2 (spacecraft) 37
Sputnik 1 (spacecraft) 10, 24-25
stars
    mapping 68-9
    searching among 70-71
    studying 66, 67
Sun 13, 52-53

T

telescopes 9, 10, 13, 64-71
thrust 17
thunderstorms 28, 29
Titan 12, 54
toilets 41
transponders 21
Tsiolkovsky, Konstantin 10

U

Universe, composition of 71

V

V-2 rockets 10
velocity 17
Venus 12, 58-59
Venus Express 12, 58-59
volcanic ash 29
Vostok 1 (spacecraft) 11
Voyager 1 (spacecraft) 11

W

water
    on Mars 56, 57
    on the Moon 13
    recycled 41
weather
    Jupiter 62
    Mars 56
    satellites 11, 19, 28-29, 31
    space 52
Webb Telescope 13, 68

Z

Zveda module (ISS) 36

Project Editor John Hort
Project Art Editor Stefan Georgiou
Senior Production Editor Jennifer Murray
Senior Production Controller Louise Minhane
Senior Acquisitions Editor Katy Flint
Design Manager Victoria Short
Managing Director Mark Searle

Designed for DK by Sarah Crookes
Written by Ben Elcomb
Illustrations copyright © Rômolo D'Hipólito

DK would like to thank Charlie Donaldson and Alisha Comber at Rocket Licensing; and Nadia Lueders and the rest of the team at ESA.

The European Space Agency is not a manufacturer or distributor of the product. ESA authorised branding of the product with the ESA name, acronym, and/or logotype. Licensed by Rocket Licensing on behalf of ESA.

First published in Great Britain in 2026 by
Dorling Kindersley Limited
20 Vauxhall Bridge Road,
London SW1V 2SA

The authorised representative in the EEA is
Dorling Kindersley Verlag GmbH. Arnulfstr. 124,
80636 Munich, Germany

Copyright © 2026 Dorling Kindersley Limited
A Penguin Random House Company
10 9 8 7 6 5 4 3 2 1
001-348767-Mar/2026

All rights reserved.
No part of this publication may be reproduced, stored in or introduced into a retrieval system, or transmitted, in any form, or by any means (electronic, mechanical, photocopying, recording, or otherwise), without the prior written permission of the copyright owner.
DK values and supports copyright. Thank you for respecting intellectual property laws by not reproducing, scanning or distributing any part of this publication by any means without permission. By purchasing an authorised edition, you are supporting writers and artists and enabling DK to continue to publish books that inform and inspire readers.

No part of this publication may be used or reproduced in any manner for the purpose of training artificial intelligence technologies or systems. In accordance with Article 4(3) of the DSM Directive 2019/790, DK expressly reserves this work from the text and data mining exception.

A CIP catalogue record for this book
is available from the British Library.
ISBN: 978-0-2417-33127

Printed and bound in China

www.dk.com